TODAY'S INSPIRED LATINA™

Volume V

LIFE STORIES OF SUCCESS IN THE FACE OF ADVERSITY

JACKIE CAMACHO-RUIZ

Today's Inspired Latina

This book is a compilation of stories from numerous Latinas who have each contributed a chapter and is designed to provide inspiration to our readers.

It is sold with the understanding that the publisher and the individual authors are not engaged in the rendering of psychological, legal, accounting or other professional advice. The content and views in each chapter are the sole expression and opinion of its author and not necessarily the views of Fig Factor Media, LLC.

For more information, contact:

Today's Inspired Latina | www.todayslatina.com
Fig Factor Media, LLC | www.figfactormedia.com

Cover Design & Layout by Juan Pablo Ruiz
Printed in the United States of America

ISBN: 978-1-7330635-0-0

To all the young Latinas with big dreams and aspirations.

Contents:

Acknowledgements

As always, I would like to thank the team for their effort in putting together this amazing Volume V, especially the love of my life and creative director, Juan Pablo Ruiz and Manuel Serna for their design expertise, Karen Dix for working so closely with the authors as editor and project manager. I would also like to thank all the sponsors of the *Today's Inspired Latina* movement, especially Wintrust, who has been such a dedicated partner in our mission.

I'd also like to thank the past and present authors of *Today's Inspired Latina* for their part in elevating this movement since they first shared their story with the world, especially the authors in this volume, who bring a beautiful new energy to the project.

Finally, I would like to thank all the seeking, dreaming, young Latinas in the world who read this book and allow us to inspire them. In turn, you inspire us to be the best we can be every day.

Introduction

BY JACQUELINE CAMACHO-RUIZ

When we take leaps of faith, they sometimes lead us somewhere so special and unimaginable that all we can do is surrender to the magical energy being bestowed upon us.

That is how I feel these days.

Five years after the modest launch of the first volume of *Today's Inspired Latina*, I stand in wonder in the shadow of a true global movement of Latina empowerment. The series has now given voice to more than 132 authors across the globe and is now attracting the attention of politicians and Fortune 500 brands.

This past year, *Today's Inspired Latina* caught the attention of Estee Lauder, and a partner event in Chicago and New York resulted in an evening of magic, with participants taking home an engraved lipstick with our hashtag #ELxTIL on them. Even as we prepare Volume VI featuring European authors and set to launch in Amsterdam this fall, I am receiving calls from aspiring authors throughout the world who want to participate in Volume VII in 2020.

Hundreds of people turned out for our first ever, live LatinaTalks in 2019, featuring presentations from our authors. With 43 of our authors based in New York, The New York Times, who has hosted book launches for us the past two years, has asked to host an east coast LatinaTalks at their office! That will make Today's Inspired Latina one of the premier events for Hispanic

Heritage month in NYC! There is also a proclamation in the works for "Today's Inspired Latina Day" in Chicago, planned national television spots, and the magic goes on and on!

Most amazing of all, though, is the appreciation I have received from the authors who have thanked me for providing them with a family, a like-minded sisterhood that works towards Latina empowerment. We are united in our support for one another.

In short, I breathe deeply in gratitude, for this was not the plan, but all a gift from the universe that I must humbly accept. I don't know what else the universe has in store for me, but I stand here with open arms, waiting to embrace it all!

Jacqueline Camacho-Ruiz
Entrepreneur, Author, Speaker, Philanthropist, Pilot, Founder of Today's Inspired Latina

Preface

BY ROMMY PENNELLA

Executive Director, New York Cosmetology Chamber

When we hear the word "Latina," what comes to mind is being proud, loved, and empowered. Being a Latina is about leadership, courage, being fierce, and having a sense that we can do it all.

Every day, the culture and the beauty of being Latina encourages me to become successful, as the first generation of immigrant parents from Ecuador and Honduras. My parents strengthen my mindset because if they made it in this country, rising from nothing to something despite their language barrier, I can do the same.

I would like to congratulate Jackie Camacho-Ruiz for creating this extraordinary book that presents many different, powerful Latinas telling their stories to the next generation. These stories bring hope, wisdom, and encouragement.

I have always pushed hard against the stereotypes faced by women and particularly, Latinas. At Fordham University, I opened the first Marketing Society with the highest number of members in the school. I helped many students obtain corporate jobs, and I was involved in school activities. When the moment came to announce who was nominated for the class Leadership Award, I found out I was nominated, along with four other students. I was the only Latina. The other students were featured in the school newspaper, but not me. I was very disappointed, but that didn't stop me. I kept going. My mom told me to not worry what people thought about me and to be proud of what I had done for the school and for others. Graduation day came, and everyone was eager to find out who the big leader was in our class of 236 students. The Dean looked at me and said, "Leadership is not counted by popularity. Leadership is being responsible for paving the path for others through selfless acts that empower and strengthen them on their journey. I and my colleagues all find that in Rommy Pennella!"

That moment was special for me, engraved in my heart, and made me realize that everything is possible. I've always felt that Latinas are a different breed, with superpowers to make things happen.

After college, I had a line of job offerings from great corporations. I have worked for many large corporations including IBM, Kraft Foods and Ogilvy & Mather. I was driven to learn every aspect of management, brand development, and industry specific processes. I was praised for my outstanding work because I knew I had to compete. I knew I would be looked at as a stereotype, so I felt I had to work ten times harder. You can't give up on obstacles, because you will find obstacles in all parts of life. The biggest reward is when you succeed because you never gave up.

Throughout the years, I wanted very much to be a part of a movement to help my Latino community to feel fearless and accomplish their dreams. Therefore, my mom, Charito Cisneros, and I created the New York Hispanic Cosmetology & Beauty Chamber of Commerce, the first Beauty Chamber of Commerce in the United States with members nationwide and even from Puerto Rico, the Dominican Republic, Ecuador, Colombia, and Argentina. We wanted to assist those in the beauty industry with language barriers to become small business owners and entrepreneurs with licenses or employees at Fortune 500 beauty companies. Our organization creates so many opportunities, especially to those who have lost hope.

One Colombian woman, who is an engineer in her country, came to the United States with her eight-year-old child. Her boyfriend pampered her with all that comes with the American dream. However, the dream was destroyed when he left her for another woman, essentially leaving her with her child at a shelter. She came to our office with the hope of becoming a makeup artist. She figured it was a short-term career where she could make some money. However, my eagerness to support this young Latina woman and empower her to achieve her dreams pushed me to give her a grant for beauty school. It was a challenge for both of us, not only because of the language barrier, but also because she felt that she wouldn't make it. I told her, "You are a Latina. You are powerful. You are a mother. You are fearless. Show that to your son!"

With that, she finished her school coursework and got her license. Now she is the owner of two beauty salons with 12 chairs and employees working for her. It was a great feeling of accomplishment for her when we cut the inauguration ribbon. In addition, she is working towards a degree in management and has a MWBE (Minority Woman Business Enterprise) certification. Her son even calls me "Titi Rommy" because he thinks, like I do, that we are family.

We are Latinas and we are family. We encourage one another to push forward for our culture and our community. We need to encourage each other to succeed. I have won many different awards including the Small Business Administration "Women Champion of the Year." I have opened 119 businesses in one year with a Proclamation of the City and received citations from governors to senators. But nothing is more rewarding than helping others accomplish their dream. Nothing can stop us, because WE ARE LATINA and WE ARE POWERFUL!

Thania Keppel

"Life gives us what we need to grow into the best version of ourselves."

For the first 33 years of my life, I felt awkward. I was like the weirdo that didn't fit in. I attribute my struggles and challenges to feelings of rejection that stem from my father. He was very proud when my brother was born but never expressed pride in me. This made me feel like a failure, which defined my life for many, many years.

Because I felt unwanted, I was in competition with the men of the world, in every area of life, every single day. I needed to prove that I was as good as all of them. I wanted so badly to be loved, to be good enough, to belong, no matter what the cost. Instead of being who I was, I did whatever I needed to do to fit into a family that I thought didn't want me. In the process, I found that the fear of not being loved and the fear of being rejected can become the fear of not being good enough. This can lead us to please others, rather than be ourselves.

As a result, I stopped being a tender, sweet girl. I became the competitive, aggressive, macho girl that could beat anyone, just to be good enough, so my parents could feel proud of me. It didn't seem to work. I never felt like I was "enough," and I ended up isolating myself from my family and the world. I didn't want anybody to get to know me because I didn't want anyone to be disappointed in me. My life turned into an exhausting power struggle between who I was and who I felt I should be.

I couldn't see any of this until my life was totally miserable and falling apart. Striving to be someone else actually ruined my first marriage, harming my ex-husband, my kids, and myself in the process. I realized I had to do something about it or die of depression.

THE AWAKENING

Turning the page requires courage, because it brings lots of anxiety, risk, fear, and uncertainty. For me, it meant losing everything. When I left my husband, I was living in an empty house, sleeping on an air mattress, covering myself and my kids with coats and jackets, and using eating utensils from McDonald's. Only when you are willing to lose everything can you gain it all. I wasn't going back, and I was willing to face my dragons. That was the moment I had an awakening.

It took me years to get there. Through coaching sessions, reading self-help books, and practicing acceptance and forgiveness, I gradually figured out what I really wanted. It was as if someone had pulled back the curtain and I was now able to see how empty and hollow my life had been. What a revelation! Having a coach changed my life; I became a believer. Where I once felt lost, guilty, and ashamed, I was now lovingly guided, without any judgement. My mentors and coaches were there to support me. I realized that we are never alone.

I also found Waldorf Education, which was more than just an education for my children, but also a spiritual, nourishing path for me to heal through art and nature. I fell in love with anthroposophy, the science that supports Waldorf Education.

Learning what it feels like to jump off the cliff of uncertainty allowed me to discover my mission. Finally, I had found my purpose. I wanted to be there for those willing to have it all, like a container, or a cocoon for them to become a beautiful butterfly, even if they didn't know how to transform. I wanted to show them the way. I wanted to show them that they needn't be afraid, because they would not be alone; a sisterhood would be there for them. If they jumped off the cliff, someone would catch them.

We were given this life because we are strong enough to live it and the right people will show up at the perfect moment. If I could do it, so can you!

All the inner work that I have gone through, the pain, the struggle, and the challenges were all there for me to fulfill my purpose. I created the "BeYOUtiful and Powerful" experiential workshop, the "30 Days to the Best Version of Yourself" online program and the "Antisabotage program," with which I am helping women start from scratch to develop a new vision for themselves. I'm helping them love, respect, and honor who they really are and recover their self-esteem and their core power to embrace their uniqueness, just as I did.

Interestingly enough, the more I teach, the more I'm

healed and the more I accept and embrace myself. The more I embrace that I am no longer a weirdo but living the transition from weird-awkward-different to authentic-amazingly-unique, the more joyful my life becomes. I feel appreciation and gratitude for all the events that have happened to me in the past because they are the foundation of the woman that I am today and my ability to inspire and support others in making a transition #FromVictimToPowerful.

Some of you might say, "Well, I'm not feeling that powerful right now. I am struggling with an issue." We all face challenges. However, the bigger the struggle and the bigger the obstacles, the stronger and wiser our spirit grows and the faster we can become the best version of ourselves.

Circumstances are always there. They don't just happen TO us, they also happen FOR us. Every challenge that life presents is an opportunity to grow stronger, bolder, and to experience life with a new level of awareness.

SERVICE AND MOVEMENTS

When an earthquake shook Mexico in 2017, I was already living in the U.S. because I wanted my kids to experience Waldorf Education all the way into high school. Mexico only offers Waldorf Education through middle school, so I burned my bridges, followed my passion, and came to Santa Fe, New Mexico so they could attend the Santa Fe Waldorf High School.

Living in the U.S. didn't change my love and gratitude for my home country. I knew that I could do something more than just "pray for Mexico." Now that I was freed from my personal drama bubble, I could look outside of my own life, help others, and impact the world. I became a channel of communication through Facebook and WhatsApp. To do even more, I managed to send first aid equipment to the rescuers and 40 tons of aid to Oaxaca, Mexico. I even wrote an e-book, *"Despierta Mexico Esta Temblando"* (Wake Up, Mexico is Trembling), as a fundraiser to continue helping victims of these kind of tragedies in the future.

I have been healing my inner awkwardness every day through serving others. The more I make a difference in somebody else's life, the more my life has meaning and the more unstoppable I become. My dad always said, "If you don't live to serve, it serves nobody that you live." Giving is the mindset of champions! Successful people understand that giving is receiving. Giving other people the possibility of expanding their horizons has expanded mine too.

The #metoo movement has been a wake-up call for many women to stop hiding and instead express their pain, be seen and heard, and begin to heal. Oprah started the #TimesUp movement to stop the abuse, the indignity, the feeling that we deserve to be treated badly, the feelings of shame and guilt, and instead compel women to say "NO" more often. Transformation happens when we stop what doesn't serve us anymore, and these movements encourage us to eliminate such things from our lives.

Today, I want to invite you to take the next step, the one that can give us power and strength from within. The time has arrived to change the conversation--our inner conversation. We need to stop the small talk in our heads that judges and criticizes us every single day.

In an attempt to give hope and a new perspective to women, I started a movement in which adversity, circumstances, and our past become the platform for our future, not a definition of who we are. Let us be stronger than our circumstances, choosing self-forgiveness and acceptance, and planting the seed of greatness in our hearts and minds. Life doesn't always give us what we want; it gives us what we need to grow into the best version of ourselves.

#IAPPRECIATEMYSELF MOVEMENT

Creating powerful habits of self-appreciation brought me back to my self-esteem, my power, my greatness. I invite you to join me in the #IAppreciateMyself movement, in which we recognize and embrace the value and power that comes from our feminine essence, not an unauthentic, masculine model of how women should be.

The #IAppreciateMyself movement includes a challenge to complete a list of ten qualities or actions every day that bring value to either your life or the life of someone else. The movement offers ten reasons to celebrate your wonderfulness and embrace your value as a human being.

The second part of the movement is to be witnessed in your transformation and stop hiding in the shadows. Instead, be free to show that what you do and who you are is meaningful. Letting the world know that you are valuable is a beautiful way to heal. Despite the possibility of being criticized or judged, those who dare to be seen should be celebrated. They have become an inspiration as their self-esteem is slowly, but steadily, recovered. A soft empowerment happens. I dare you to try it.

While expanding the movement for men to honor and appreciate women, I met Jackie Camacho. As an experiment, I asked ten men to accept the challenge of creating a list of 10 women for 10 days, listing 10 qualities that they appreciate in them. The participating 10 men then challenged 10 other men to do the same, to continue growing the movement and make women feel appreciated. My brother had Jackie on his list as a wonderful human being who is caring, giving, and powerful. She experienced the power of being acknowledged for her essence, and she opened her heart and her project for me to share it with the world. Thank you, Jackie, for sharing this space with me so we can co-create the wonder and beauty of our uniqueness.

Being grateful has been an important part of my success and I want to share the power of feeling successful with everyone. Imagine that I have a crystal ball and I can show you how powerful, how amazing, and unstoppable you are, and I can see the highest expression of yourself. Are you there yet?

Let's start a new inner conversation in which we believe and allow ourselves to be respected, honored, and worshipped as the divine creatures that we are. For me, it only happened in my life when it happened in my mind. The first step was to discover that all change starts within and I needed to be the first one to love and respect myself. I needed to believe that I had learned to be strong, perseverant, daring, and assertive as a result of the pain I suffered earlier in life. When you are brave enough to own your power, make peace with your past, and let it all go, you will finally be ready to access your uniqueness. When forgiveness touches your heart, you will realize you are unique, amazing, and unstoppable... just like ME!

REFLECTION

1. What are the blessings that pain and struggle have given you?
2. What are the lessons that you have learned because of your circumstances?
3. What if you could transform from a victim into a proudly successful survivor who empowers and helps others to overcome their struggles?

BIOGRAPHY

"Committed to your success" is Thania Keppel's mindset and mantra. She holds your hand to show you a new path towards growth and fulfillment.

Born and raised in Mexico City, Thania has worked in the coaching industry for more than 12 years. After seeking her own answers, she discovered that personal growth is the key to opening doors to the ideal life that every human being is destined to live.

Passionate about Waldorf Education, she moved to Santa Fe, New Mexico to obtain a Waldorf high school education for her two boys. Along the way, she found love and got remarried to a very supportive and loving man.

Thania is an enthusiastic, active, Commercial Real Estate Coach. She is considered an expert in brand positioning in Mexico City and is a life strategist, mother, wife, and author of the Amazon bestselling ebook, *Despierta México Está Temblando*" and the social movement, #IAppreciateMyself as well as #letschangetheconversation and #fromvictimtopowerful.

Thania, the "Freedom Coach," is certified as a passion test facilitator and in biography work. She has created her own programs and workshops in English and Spanish and passionately devotes her time and energy to inspire and be the change needed in the world.

Thania Keppel
thaniakeppel@gmail.com
www.thaniakeppel.com
(505) 982-0906

Macarena Tamayo-Calabrese

"There will be moments that define you; in those moments, be your best advocate."

Children from Latina households are taught to respect authority without question, especially our family and teachers. I grew up hearing, "Macarena, when you walk out that door, you walk out with my reputation, my mother's reputation, and her mother's reputation. Each of us has cared for and watched over it. It's your turn. I expect you to return home with it intact." My mother's directive was to never get in trouble or be disrespectful at school, or I wouldn't live another day!

MEETING GOLIATH

I was a quiet kid who lived in a predominantly white suburb and was trying to simultaneously manage being a new immigrant, an American teen, and the English language. For example, why was the word "always" spelled with one "L" when it meant "all ways?" Why can't a freak use the sports hallway at school? I was neither, so what hallway should I use?

As for applying to college, my immigrant parents were limited in their ability to help so I visited my counselor, a petite woman resembling a vanilla version of June Cleaver. When she asked about my plans after graduation, I proudly replied, "I want to be a lawyer." Politely, she suggested that if I was interested in law, I should consider becoming a paralegal. Being naïve, I was confused.

Suddenly, I realized what was happening. Discrimination had been lurking behind that desk, awaiting its prey. Before I could react, it bit me and I was paralyzed. Every emotion rushed me—from self-doubt to rage. Do I walk out? Do I protest? And there she sat with a pleasant smirk, waiting for me to acquiesce. I wanted to retaliate, but she was an authority figure. What if she called my mom?

There are moments that define us, and this was one of mine. She was my Goliath and a David dwelled within me. Years before, when I told my mother that I wasn't as smart as the other kids in school because I was a minority, she exploded. "How dare you disrespect our entire family and heritage! You come from amazing places and a tenacious people!" she cried.

She explained we are a minority in number, but my Spanish and Ecuadorian family heritage was enough. God does not apportion intelligence, valor, tenacity, or grit geographically. He does not say United States *yes*; Spain and Ecuador, *no*. First world countries *yes*; third world countries *no*. Then she said the words I live by today, "Some will try to put you down or make you feel like you are less, so you must be *faster, smarter, stronger, and tougher."*

Trying to be respectful, I asked the counselor what a paralegal did, still hoping I had misunderstood.

"Can I represent clients and go to court?"

"No, but you can help the lawyers that do that."

"Why would I want to do that, when I can go to court and be the one to present all the work I prepared?"

"Because you would be the paralegal."

"Who can be the lawyers then?"

We continued until shaken, frightened, angry, and in tears I said, "I want to be a lawyer, not a paralegal." She told me to go to community college and get a paralegal degree first; then see if I could go further. She told me unless I followed her plan, she would not help me with applications or provide a letter of recommendation. Still crying, I told her I would become a lawyer without her help and walked out. I never got a letter from her, but I did become a lawyer!

It's been decades since that day, but I still feel the same pit in my stomach when I think about it. There will be moments that define you; in those moments, be your best advocate. If you encounter Goliath, be your own David—one dwells within you.

Stay at the forefront of your own life. I didn't know it then, but I wasn't fighting for a letter or a degree; I was fighting to determine who I was going to be and the kind of life I was going to live.

PASSION FOR ADVOCACY

Why am I so passionate about advocacy? Because the life we

lead and society we build depends on it. It's how we determine the human experience and what we deliver to future generations.

Of course, advocacy goes hand in hand with leadership. Today, we're flooded with every kind of leadership training program, podcast, webinar, and certification. On stage, with a commanding presence, leaders address their audiences in perfectly tailored power suits or runway-inspired, relaxed-fit jeans, and tennis shoes. We are amazed by their cutting-edge presentations and deep thoughts.

In reality, leadership is a muddy, murky, lonely place. By definition, leaders clear the path in the dark jungles of our minds, but first they stumble in shadowy, unfamiliar places. They grapple with their deepest fears; they consider giving up, experience failure, and seek to atone with their faith and deepest convictions.

Why talk about the lonely and painful side of leadership? Because these forks in the road ultimately open new worlds or send us down a rabbit hole. At these critical junctures, you find grit, resiliency, tenacity, and above all, faith. Empowered by them, you will seek justice, freedom, and opportunity. Advocacy is needed to cultivate and grow everything.

So, who are you? Are you the change agent and edge-walker? Not everyone should be, or we'd be living in a heck of a mess. For me, I'm most comfortable experiencing change and walking on the edge. Advocacy—a natural outgrowth of both— has been my constant companion as a lawyer.

I vividly remember the man who desperately begged me to meet with him on a Saturday evening. He lived in Texas and his wife had left in the middle of the night with their eight-year-old daughter. He found her because the child was in the hospital and the mother called him for money to pay the bill. The hospital told him that the man who had fled with the mother had molested the daughter. Mom was in denial.

Every Thursday, he drove from Texas to Illinois to see his daughter for a three-hour visit on Saturday mornings. After the visit, he would drive back to Texas for work on Monday. We finally got the judge to grant his request to remove the child from Illinois and return home with her dad. That child became a straight "A" student. Dad remarried, and she went on to college.

I also practiced immigration law. Today, three sisters and two very relieved parents are U.S. citizens. Because of a mishandled case, the girls had landed in federal prison. Their crime? Getting a part-time job to help their parents pay the bills. All three are now productive U.S. citizens with jobs and families.

A case I will carry with me always was that of an excited young couple expecting their baby daughter. Unfortunately, the baby was born with a terminal tumor protruding from the back of her head and would not live long. Concurrently, the time to process the father's U.S. visa arrived and he went to the U.S. embassy in his native country as required. There, he was turned down on a technicality, meaning he could not re-enter the U.S. for ten years. We petitioned for a special entry visa to allow him to be with his child, who would soon die in the hospital, but he was turned away at the border twice.

I cried and felt I had failed. Finally, I turned to Washington, appealed the decision, and it was approved! He legally entered the U.S., headed to the hospital and held his baby as he saw her take her last breath. Afterwards, we were able to reopen his case, reprocess the visa, and obtain permanent residency. With time, the couple had other children.

I am also passionate about advocating for the rule of law itself because it provides the privilege of living peacefully in a free society despite our differences. The rule of law is always at risk and never a given. I was lucky to work at the American Bar Association for 15 years and learn from the best that words are powerful, the pen is mighty, and the voices behind them matters. If you complain about the laws, imagine if there were none, or if our legal system did not evolve with us.

Lawyers on several continents taught me that the struggle to create, foster, and grow a free society continues. I met an admirable African, female lawyer who had been repeatedly imprisoned for her work defending human rights. As executive director for the National Association of Women Lawyers in 2012, I met with the first-ever, generation of women lawyers in a Middle Eastern nation. Most were young women who were routinely dismissed with the wave of a hand by male judges as they approached the bench. They were told to go home and tend house, as their case would not be heard. They could not even share experiences because organized groups of any sort were illegal. They practiced law in loneliness, desperation, and fear.

I also directed several anti-trafficking projects abroad. Trafficked girls were routinely dismissed as mere prostitutes and safe houses didn't want them. We worked to raise the age of sexual consent and witnessed several prosecutors targeted by organized crime for bringing "johns" and traffickers to trial.

HISTORY'S FOOTSTEPS

But what about failure? How do we avoid it? We don't. Failure lives with leadership in the same muddy, murky, and lonely place. It is important. Plan on it and plan for it. We grow best when we feel uncomfortable and pressured. Failure is the marker for new beginnings, never a destination. As for advocacy, it's not always about winning; it's about showing up, making the argument, and helping others connect with the issue. It's about creating empathy or the need for change.

In my career, I also learned to recognize opportunities, prepare for them, and pursue them. Be open-minded and remember that each of the experiences, jobs, and adventures is a deposit in your life's bank. Eventually, you'll cash in on them with dividends.

In 2014, I was ready for a change. I knew I wanted to stop traveling abroad, spend more precious time with my daughters, and ditch the near two-hour commute downtown. Surfing the vast ocean of online job sites, I came across the job posting for my current position—President & CEO of Naper Settlement, a living history museum. I dismissed it several times, but it gnawed at me. Finally, I opened it.

The job description called for someone who understood nonprofits, had experience in transformative work, expertise in management, working with boards, budgets, grants, and developing a vision and institutional plan for the future (my specialty!). Above all, they sought someone who understood the importance of honoring the museum's past and could advocate for its bright, fruitful future. Perfect! I cashed in all my dividends and the national search ended.

Today, I am the President and CEO of Naper Settlement and its greatest advocate. History museums are the keepers of our collective stories; they are the teaching meccas for future generations. They are living, breathing, entities with an often overlooked soul and purpose. Like my former clients, they need advocacy.

Science, politics, medicine, etc. all grow, improve, and develop by standing on the wide shoulders of history. History museums teach everything from organic matter to why you matter. If we are not there to preserve, share, and derive lessons from history, who will?

But why advocate? Why show up for the fight? Because this is how you *become faster, smarter, stronger, and tougher.* Imagine if I had acquiesced that day in high school. Who would I be today? Who would have gotten that child back to her father? Who would have sought a safe house for trafficked girls? Where would those three sisters be? We build a powerful future when we collectively advocate for a brighter tomorrow.

REFLECTION

1. Who was your first Goliath? What gave you the strength to face him/her? What have you taken from it?

2. What things do you need to be at the forefront of your life?

3. What deposits are you making in your bank of life?

BIOGRAPHY

Macarena Tamayo-Calabrese is the President and CEO of Naper Settlement, a nationally accredited and leading history museum.

She has 25 years of law experience including 15 years with American Bar Association (ABA), directing the International Liaison Office and the Latin America and Caribbean Law Initiative. She implemented several rule of law projects for democracies on criminal and human rights issues and training programs for government officials in Africa and China.

While practicing immigration law, she served on the liaison committee for the American Immigration Lawyers Association's (AILA) Department of Homeland Security's Office of Chief Counsel. She was Chair-elect for the Illinois State Bar Association's (ISBA) International and Immigration Law Section and appointed to the ABA Commission on Immigration's Advisory Committee and the advisory board of its magazine, Perspectives. As the Executive Director of the National Association of Women Lawyers, Macarena was one of only six Latinas to head a national association.

She is a contributing author of *Dear Sisters, Dear Daughters: Strategies for Success from Multicultural Women Attorneys* and is Chair of the Diversity Committee for the Chicago Bar Association.

Macarena graduated from Hofstra School of Law in New York. She and her husband, Michael, have three daughters and own a law firm.

Macarena Tamayo-Calabrese
calabresem@naperville.il.us
(630) 675-0486

Marcela Avila

"Failure only occurs if you stop trying."

It was 1994 and I had just earned my degree in graphic design from Ecuador. I was enjoying the opportunity to study at Stanford University in California and was trying to come up with a theme for my final project in a film class. I remember how hard it was for me to find something with a powerful message that would have an impact on the audience and myself. I had many ideas with commercial or narrative overtones, but it was not until I heard the story of José, a Central American engineer who worked as a gardener at the university, that I decided the topic for my project.

José was a professional who immigrated to the U.S., leaving everything behind to get a better future for his children. His story was filled with sacrifice, suffering, and conviction. I decided to make a documentary about him called "An American Dream," never knowing that 25 years later, my very own family and I would be living out a similar story!

JOY AND TEARS IN ECUADOR

I was born in the United States and am the youngest of

three daughters born to a Mexican mother and Ecuadorian father. Because my father's job kept us moving, I had the opportunity to live in and travel to many different countries. My parents raised me to be a good person with solid, moral values. To this day, they are constantly guiding me along with every member of the family.

In Japan, I studied TV production at NHK – Japan. When I returned to Ecuador to work as a television producer, I met Silvio, my husband. Together we have walked together the last 24 years, raising our two wonderful children. Over the years, we have undertaken different projects together, always with the belief that everything is possible if you try hard enough.

In Ecuador, I worked extensively in television production, creating and planning several popular national shows. As an event planner, I organized and executed private and commercial events like the largest automotive show ever held in Ecuador and endorsed by Ferrari. I also opened a unique store, party venue, and cooking school where I planned many personalized parties with great success.

I was in my sixth month of pregnancy with my first daughter when my gynecologist told us that her growth was stunted, and she would be born with some type of syndrome. The news was devastating. I cried for days. Every time someone asked me about my pregnancy, I would cry and imagine all the situations that my little girl would have to endure in life with some sort of special need. I was looking for explanations and I thought that maybe I had done something wrong. The doctor requested a number of tests and we spent what little money we had on them.

We were in the hospital about to start one of the many tests when I was asked to sign a release form in case I lost the baby in the process. When I read that, I was so upset that we decided we were done with testing. It was a turning point that made us realize that we had to accept reality and prepare ourselves for what would probably be the biggest challenge of our lives.

My daughter was the most important thing to us. I felt the unconditional love of a mother and since then, I knew that my children and my husband are, and always will be, the most important part of my life. We sought a second opinion from a new gynecologist. Months later, my daughter María José was born. She was completely healthy!

We were overjoyed and our decision to make family the priority in our lives became even stronger. My second pregnancy was a little delicate and I had some complications. Despite them, after experiencing a normal pregnancy full of unnecessary fears, I was able to enjoy it this time. I did have to go to the hospital several times with the possibility of losing my son. However, with the positive attitude and expert guidance of the doctor, our son Miguel was born healthy and strong.

Our children's education has always been important to us. María José started her college life in one of the best universities in the country. In his high school years, Miguel began to stand out on his swim team in one of the most prestigious clubs in Ecuador.

THE DECISION

Silvio had opened a communications company in Ecuador which generated work and supported families for more than 15 years. I have always admired his entrepreneurial spirit, creativity, and work ethic.

Meanwhile, Ecuador's economic situation, like many other Latin American countries, began to decline. It affected everyone. We looked for loans and applied for scholarships and financial aid for my daughter's college but because of the government's problems, we couldn't find assistance.

We started paying all the bills with our savings. We decided to start small parallel businesses which did not require an upfront investment. We sold fruit pulp and had important clients in restaurants and hotels. I created and delivered promotional packages. Although the extra income helped, it was just not enough.

Silvio struggled to save the company, the workers and in a way, our lifestyle. It became very hard for me to obtain a full-time job, so I welcomed every little bit of income I could.

Silvio always said that in Ecuador we could achieve what we set out to do. At first, he rejected the idea of immigrating elsewhere, realizing how difficult it would be. However, I never wanted to completely rule it out.

We were familiar with immigration. Silvio's brother left Ecuador in the late 1990's and my sister did the same at the beginning of the year 2000 during one of the country's biggest crises. My sister Chacha (a nickname) and her family settled in a Chicago suburb, in the same area where I repeated my senior year in high school as an exchange student. She never missed any opportunity to encourage us to come to the U.S.

For a long time, we did not see any reason to leave Ecuador. Most of our families and friends were there, our children were receiving a good education and we had a business, a nice house, and led a comfortable life. Crises bring instability and can be devastating if you don't know how to handle them, but they can also bring opportunities.

After many long, terrible nights filled with tears and arguments, we made the decision to immigrate to the country where I was born. It was not an easy decision, but we knew it would give our children broader horizons and new opportunities for us all, even though we expected to face challenges and make sacrifices in our new country.

In August 2016, filled with illusions and fears, we arrived at my sister's house with eight suitcases in tow. We spent two long years with Chacha and her husband Marco and we cannot thank them enough because without their hospitality, we would not have our new life. But as grateful as we are, it is also disheartening when you try to move forward and things do not work out as planned.

ADJUSTING TO AMERICA

The process of adjusting to our new home was different for everyone. Miguel was a senior in high school and didn't know anyone at his new school. María José started college again and began to work for the first time. Our children's growth and achievement was our motivation to keep going every day.

Silvio came here to study the language and began to search for opportunities. I had to find a new job. Above all, I had to stay strong and encourage everybody, even though I was disappointed that my experience and knowledge seemed to have no value in my new environment.

I spent hours in front of a computer searching for a job, waiting for the interview that never came, or hearing things like, "You have an impressive resume but …". I knew my strategy had to change so I considered new industries and jobs that could help me grow and evolve.

After applying for several positions, I accepted one in a completely different field. I thought this could help me adapt to my new country. In truth, there were times I thought I wouldn't make it. Sometimes I felt like running away but that would be failing, and in my mind, there is no room for that. It took me a while, but I finally got used to my job.

Unfortunately, going through hard times was not letting us move forward. We were trying, but things were not working out. For the first time in my life, I noticed the problems were paralyzing me. Silvio and I lost the desire to fight; we were just surviving day to day. But we also knew that we could not give up because of our two wonderful children who were showing us they could accomplish anything they wanted.

It was then that I learned about *do-over.me*, a nonprofit organization that provides support and guidance on your personal and professional life. It was the light that lit my way to change.

BRIGHTER DAYS

I realized that I may not be able to change my present reality, but I could change my attitude towards my situation. I learned how powerful it is to be grateful. I began to work on changing my mindset, thinking positively, and as a result I learned that I am the only person that can control my own happiness. I connected with wonderful, positive people and little by little things started to brighten up.

Today, we are in a process of reinvention. Silvio and I formed 593 Marketing, Inc., a business which combines all our experience and knowledge. It is a small company that is beginning to take shape. While Silvio works the business, I have earned a certification as an event planner and work two other positions. María José is achieving her goals by her own merits and she has transferred to the university she always wanted to attend. Miguel has been promoted twice in his work and is looking to transfer to a university to pursue the career of his dreams. As a mother, I cannot be prouder to see my kids accomplish their goals and work towards their aspirations.

I am a person who tries to take action even when I am afraid and overly anxious. I think things happen for a reason. Even if I cannot understand the reason behind what is happening to me at the moment, there will be a time when I will understand why things happened the way they did. I trust that God will guide me to make the right decisions.

I must admit that I do not like failure because for me it is equivalent to giving up. We can all have falls and make mistakes.

We can try several times to achieve a goal, and along the way we can change our mind and learn new things. Falls will always teach us something, but failure only occurs if you stop trying. For me, failure should never be an option.

I'm nowhere near where I thought I would be at this stage in my life. Adversity can be the opportunity life gives us to flourish. Maybe adversity is not an obstacle, but a step to take us forward on our path. Starting over can be a difficult and painful process, but we must be open to learning new things. Of course, there will be ups and downs, and there is still a lot to do and many new opportunities to come. We are just starting out on this journey, and it is in our power to be the authors of a great, new story.

REFLECTION

1. Have you ever had to "start over" in life? What did it feel like?
2. Do you see adversity as obstacle or opportunity?
3. What do you do when you cannot change your situation?

BIOGRAPHY

Marcela Avila Gonzalez was born in Washington D.C. but travelled globally as a child because of her father's career. She is a graphic designer, television producer and certified wedding and event planner. She attended Stanford University, NHK-Japan, Instituto Superior de Diseño Metropolitano in Ecuador and Waubonsee Community College near Chicago.

As a television producer, she worked at several different TV stations and production companies, creating and working on important national shows with proven success. As an event planner, Marcela executed private and commercial events like the Panam GP Series sponsored by Ferrari, one of the largest automotive events held to date in Ecuador.

She also launched and operated Bee Happy, a unique store, party venue and children's cooking school in Quito that led to a business planning private parties. After discovering Do-over.me, Marcela felt the need to give back and currently serves as a volunteer Director of Philanthropy for the non-for-profit organization.

Recently, Marcela launched 593 Marketing with her husband, Silvio. She is an open-minded individual, ready to face and conquer new challenges and opportunities within her professional career. Marcela´s biggest motivation is her husband and her two children, María José and Miguel.

Marcela Avila
marcelaavila729@gmail.com
(630) 974-9163

ARE YOU EXPANDING OR EXPLODING?

Rosy D'Amico

"Take care of the energy living inside you."

Let me ask you a question. On a daily basis, do you expand or explode?

When was the last time you gave yourself a gift? Was it yesterday, a week ago, or maybe it was so long ago you don't remember? Do you want to give yourself one right now? Ok! Let's do it. All it takes is two minutes.

Be present now, open your heart and feel safe. Be aware of your breathing and the place you are. Don't do anything; just observe without judging everything. Acknowledge your emotions, thoughts, and body sensations. Do it in your own silence, with patience, love and care for yourself. Don't force it. Surrender and just be yourself.

How was it? Was it worth having a special moment for you? Did it take too long?

In this world's economy, most people are driven by hectic days, the stress of their activities and the chase for the utopic dream of giving everything to be successful in their projects or lives. We have forgotten to empower ourselves every day, free our voice, and enjoy what really matters.

BECOMING SUPERWOMAN

I was taught to be a superwoman. My mom was not the typical mother who gave everything to her daughters. She took time for herself, her husband and trips. We were simply another part of her life. She was a housewife, and, in her time, it was not important for mothers to have their own projects. I don't know if it was the right way, but she gave me a great gift in teaching me to search for my own truth, which I found several years later.

I became a housewife at the age of 20 and I raised my own family in the typical way. But on my 28th birthday, everything inside me changed.

Almost all my life I had trusted myself, but deep inside of me something was saying, "You are not completely happy." So I thought, what is missing in my life? And my mind gave a typical answer for a woman who had tried to lose weight. "Oh! I have to be thinner."

So I took some magic pills and they worked! In a few months I was *flaca* as we say in México. But a few months later, I realized that I still felt incomplete so I started taking pills again. In that moment, God or life whispered in my ear, "You don't get it!" I started to have panic attacks.

The fears that triggered my panic attacks haunted my life for many years. I was very angry and constantly asked myself, "Why?" If I was doing my best to overcome my fears, why did they continue? Did I really love life? Or was I going crazy? What was wrong with me?

Throughout my education, nobody ever taught me how my

emotions, mind, or body worked together, and I was devastated at my inability to manage my own life.

On the outside, everything looked perfect. I had two beautiful children a loving husband and a good life, but I still felt lonely.

I know that you too may have felt this volcano erupt inside of you and you have started looking for answers. With all this reconstruction inside of me, my passion emerged as my mission in life.

For me, my passion has been the energy that has driven me to study, practice and design tools that have helped me help myself. Now I use those same tools to help many people around the world.

DAILY PLAN: RENEW YOUR ENERGY

In those changing years when my first two children were little and I had to recover myself, I decided to do something radical because the version of myself as victim was not serving me well. Either I had to change or I was going to do something stupid because my inner life was fearful all day long. So I heard that voice again that told me to move, learn, and grow. However, in a contradictory way, I was very comfortable suffering so I decided to leave all the options behind. Instead, I would leave my depression behind and build a new Rosy!

I enrolled in school to pursue a master's degree in psychotherapy and studied the different techniques used by great teachers all over the world. I read hundreds of books to recover my life and I started feeling much better. But I still had the feeling that something was missing. The magic of learning only lasted a couple of days until the routine caught up with me again. I felt like I was going two steps forward and one step back. Even though I made my best effort, I didn't make lasting changes.

I still did not believe in myself until one day a voice came and asked me, "What happens if you believe in yourself without believing in yourself?" I had found my answer! I was going to pretend to be confident even though I wasn't. So I started to fake it!

As a result, two things happened. The first one was that I realized from all of my studies that everything in the universe is made of energy and we are ruled by those laws. I began to believe that we are given an amount of energy to use in our lives, plans and activities each day. Like a sponge, our energy receives all things that happen to you daily. So, you have to release and transform your energy in order to focus and create a new reality.

My second realization was that I had used my bad decisions to fuel my mind, thoughts and emotions. I had been the creator of my personal Mexican soap opera!

Meanwhile, a friend of mine started to hold a women's group on Fridays. I realized that those days my energy was great, I was motivated, and happier. What happened if I did it every day?

That moment I had a revelation that humans have renewable energy. Do you remember the middle ages when people died of the plague? It was because they didn't know anything about proper hygiene. When they learned to clean their bodies, their wounds and their houses, their physical lives improved. We do this today by brushing our teeth, taking a daily bath and getting our laundry done. These practices improve our quality of life.

But in the same way we need to take care of the energy living inside of us. I decided I had to liberate my energy everyday with exercises to renew it. My mind, emotions, and body sensations are my inner experience, so I started to clear them every day. I would let go of the problems of yesterday, visualize myself having great results, focus with actions on the activities that were essential for my day, and offer thanksgiving for a newfound reality.

Everything I learned enhanced my passion. I began renewing my energy and I became happier and more confident. I was enjoying life. I designed what I now call "Active Meditation Refresh" which provides a 16-minute tool to help you take out the garbage of your day and visualize what you want to create in life.

With this training I recovered myself. I started to give coaching to other people, then companies, and now we do it globally. But I still had my next big challenge in front of me and that was to enhance my voice in my home and with my family.

WOMEN TAKING THEIR PLACES

I was once a housewife, but when I started to grow up and become myself I wasn't the same woman anymore. I wanted to help people and give workshops around the world with my message. Even though I was happy, as soon as I got home I had to make up for my absence.

Everywhere I went I was demonstrating that I was worth it, that I loved my family, and that my methodology worked. I was like a little girl asking for approval, or someone in a race, running from one place to another. The truth was, I began to notice that instead of expanding, I was exploding as I tried to juggle my duties as a wife, working woman, and mom.

I was successful outside the home but inside, it was not very easy for my husband to have a happy woman at home who was searching outside the family for her happiness. For me, I didn't get it. Why, if I was doing good things, was he so angry and distant? I began to think we were not supposed to continue together because we viewed life differently. I felt misunderstood and lonely and he felt the same way because of my continuous change.

We started to grow apart and have different views of what we needed as a couple. I continued with "Active Meditation Refresh" every day and I visualized myself with a man who loved me as I was. Then, in a magical way, my husband started becoming a completely different man. He decided that he truly loved me and he would make me feel loved again, which he did. However, our relationship was not one-sided; I had to change some things too.

I realized that I was turning into the typical woman who searches for her dreams but ends up all alone. I didn't want that for myself. I recognized that as women we have to take our own places and have our own voice in our homes. I was not doing that; I was performing my duties, but not as my true self.

I realized that the challenge was not the panic attacks, my husband, or my job; it was me. I needed to overcome the "why?" in my head that was blocking me from the life experience I wanted. I needed to focus on expanding myself, beginning with the environment in my house. To achieve all this, I had to treat myself as another female and connect with myself every day.

For me it has been a daily challenge to feel complete, happy, and giving energy to create new relationships with every person both in my family and my work. I strive to leave behind my judgments and beliefs and focus on living the experience I deserve.

We as women empower others through our own inspiration. We nurture our environment with our energy. When I decided to become myself in my own house, it required courage to stand up and the conviction to be true to my values and presence without judging others.

WOMAN'S SECRET POWER

We have been taught to live in a man's world, hiding our true selves on the job, trading our femininity to become machines and depriving ourselves and those around us.

Our power is not in strength, competition and hurrying; our true power is in enjoying things. We do not go searching for things; we attract them. Our power center is in the womb and through enjoyment, happiness, passion, love, care and owning ourselves, we awake the female wisdom.

Women have to enjoy everything they do and it is a must in

their life, making their days powerful from its essence. You can go to a workshop, read books, have coaching sessions, or do nothing, but the only thing that will improve your quality of life is to train in loving yourself every day, becoming the unique kind of woman that you are and enjoying everything.

My life is not perfect and I have daily challenges. But I renew my energy and restart myself every day, and I have decided to believe that I experience the best moments in my life in the present day.

REFLECTION

1. Is your voice alive in your family?

2. If you had all the opportunities, what kind of women would you be?

3. What can you do to renew your energy every day?

BIOGRAPHY

Rosy D'Amico is a renewer of human energy coach who helps business owners and managers create an energy routine and increase their free time by delegating to their own teams. She works with peak performance entrepreneurs who value energy as one of their most valuable resources.

She is the author of *El Poder de Estar Contigo*, a book for people overcoming a crisis in their lives.

Rosy D'Amico has been recognized by *Forbes* for being a pioneer in introducing happiness techniques to the work environment. She has been working with more than 5,000 people in México and the U.S. teaching Active Meditation Refresh.

Rosy is CEO and designer of the Refresh Training Project, a six-week program to develop functional stress relief and leadership skills, with unique practices to prevent corporate burn out.

Rosy holds a master's degree in Ericksonian Psychotherapy and is certified as a coach by Anthony Robbins and the Greater Good Science Center at Berkeley University.

Rosy D'Amico
rosy@viverefresh.com
+52 1 (477) 700-0938

UNBRIDLED GRATITUDE FOR A LIFE OF MEANING AND SERVING OTHERS

Elena Sotomayor

"Life is a gift you earn by giving back."

It's January and I'm far from the freezing polar vortex in Chicago where I live. I'm in the Dominican Republic, walking through a beautiful path of green fields with breathtakingly majestic scenery in a true natural paradise. Here the weather is always perfect, and I'm awakened every morning by colorful birds singing outside my window. It's a place to find peace, get in touch with my soul, and reflect on my life and what's next for me.

Every morning, I wake more grateful than the last. Most importantly, I'm blessed for my health and for having the energy to get up and feel like I can conquer the world. I'm grateful for having the daily opportunity to live life to my fullest potential.

Life is a gift you earn by giving back. You give it away to others, and ironically, you receive so much more back. Life is serving those who need it most.

To some people, I seem driven by a "can do" attitude. People see me as "in charge and living life large," but just like everybody else I have had fears, insecurities, and inner demons and doubt. I have struggles with success and failure. But the most important thing I have learned is you don't go through life alone.

An immigrant arrives with a vision of endless possibilities, but you need a community to support that dream. Immigrants are forced to create and that is why we succeed. I believe everyone needs to have a shoulder to cry on, a solid ear to hear you and someone who will tell you the truth no matter how you will respond and totally accept you for who you are and who you can become. For me, that person was my mother.

DREAMS AND DECISIONS

I was born and raised in Bogota, Colombia in a great family with hard working parents. They gave us a solid foundation of education, the typical immigrant work ethic, and enough common sense to get us through life. My dad was a self-made architect who left home when my grandfather told him architecture was for the "others;" he returned six years later as an architect to prove him wrong. My mother was a dentist who gave up a very successful career and practice of her own for a "better life" in the United States for my sister and me after my parents separated. She then opened a nursery serving 20 kids every day. I never saw anyone work so hard!

As a child, I was a very active tomboy and a leader in my own strange neighborhood. My safe haven was comprised of a tight-knit community where all the neighbors knew and loved each other and my entire family, including my grandma and my aunt, lived in the same four-story building. My sister called me her mentor and I loved that responsibility.

My special place was the Caballo Blanco (White Horse),

my imaginary castle in my favorite tree that I used to climb in a nearby forest. When I returned to it after leaving the country for a few years, it looked like a beaten-up Joshua tree, smaller than I remembered, and its green leaves had yellowed like an elder pine tree going through menopause. In that tree, I had dreamed of becoming an actress and going to Hollywood, but leaving my country was something I could never imagine. It seemed so distant, but a girl can dream, and I did!

When I was nine years old, my biggest fear was that my parents would separate, or I would lose one of them in some horrible way. I imagined it every day and felt vulnerable. Then one day, I walked into the bathroom where my beautiful mother was getting ready for work. "You, me, and your sister are moving downstairs!" she declared. Then she put on red heels and a lot of very thick waterproof mascara, a trick to hide the crumbling world inside her.

At first, I couldn't understand what was happening. "What do you mean 'downstairs'?" I asked. Then I understood; my parents were divorcing, and we were moving to another unit in the building. At first, I thought it was my fault, so I started thinking about how I could fix it. I decided I wasn't going to do anything at all. Literally. I stopped showering, eating, and behaving. I decided to rebel until they got back together! I became a depressed and withdrawn little girl. That's all children can do when their foundation is shaken and mine was shaken to its core.

One day, my mother decided it was time to move to the U.S.

to take a course in orthodontics and do something progressive in her field. Her decision separated us from our immediate family and compromised her career, but she knew it was for the best and could taste the opportunity for her daughters. She had a vision and I had a dream. Even though she would suffer working at a daycare to put us through school, she was prepared to do it.

THE OPPORTUNITIES

I was transplanted from warm Colombia where everyone was either a friend or a neighbor to cold Chicago, where I lived with my mother's friend. Walking long distances to school in the freezing cold was terrible. I missed my dad, my aunt, my grandmother and my friends. I missed my tree and White Caballo. I also disliked my homeroom teacher's onion breath, the dry burgers in the lunchroom, and the flavorless food, but I knew I had to adapt so I did, as quickly as I could.

I even ran for student council president to have a say in school matters. I had a heavy accent—not Sophia Vergara heavy—but heavy enough. I worked to lose it and I did. I was not afraid of change.

I decided I was going to live life to the fullest and even take some small or stupid risks every day. I was going to be accountable for my own decisions and learn from them for the rest of my life. I saw my life as a gift I could control, and I had my mother's example of hard work and sacrifice. I couldn't let her down; I had to take advantage of the opportunity I was given.

Eventually, my mom remarried, and I had to adjust to a new

family. It was challenging, but also fun. I felt less isolated and I had a great new family who had my back.

I enrolled at UIC Chicago to study kinesiology, but soon transferred to communications and marketing with a minor in Spanish. I worked full-time while in school to help my mom. It was difficult but developed my great worth ethic.

During the last year of college, I had an internship at Fox News in Chicago. It was a requirement to graduate, and I met some folks who introduced me to the entertainment industry. This opportunity changed my life, as did an event in August of 1994. Henry Cardenas, current CEO of Cardenas Marketing Network (CMN) and now my husband, offered me a part-time job at CFA, a unique entertainment company. I first worked in accounting to learn the business, then moved into events, account management, project management, office management, then sponsorships and business development, road managing, and everything under that sun.

My dream of moving to Hollywood and becoming an actress remained, but I was now in love with a wonderful man and Chicago too. I had built a home, had friends and didn't want to leave my family. If you have a dream or a vision that is strong enough, sometimes geography is not a problem, because Hollywood came to me. One day, through my curiosity and willingness to succeed, I got lucky and met a random producer and writer from Hollywood, Rick Najera, who wanted to produce a comedy show in Chicago. He was an immigrant with no local friends or family. I decided to help however I could at no cost. I even let the cast from Los Angeles live at my home.

Our live comedy show, *Latinologues*, had a successful two-year run. Within a year, I was flying every other week to tape the show in LA. When we recorded a live taping at the Ricardo Montalban Theatre, we were asked to do a six-month run off-Broadway, which I helped finance and produce. The show eventually made it onto Broadway, with Eugenio Derbez, Jimmy Smits, Jamie Camil, Fernando Corrillo, Jacob Vargas, and yours truly in the cast!

I loved being on stage and played multiple roles. I loved the rush, the butterflies, and the nerve-wracking seconds before stepping on stage which all paid off when everyone in the room burst out laughing and forgot about their real life. I was able to take them to another place even just for a few minutes. I realized that acting brought pleasure to others by showing them "life not as it is, but as it should be." My passion for acting evolved into the business side and I discovered a talent for producing.

Rick said sometimes you find people who believe more in you than you do in yourself. For Rick, I was that person, just as my mother was that person for me.

CARING FOR OTHERS + MYSELF

All of these experiences led me to the Maestro Cares Foundation. In 1996, we traveled to the Dominican Republic for work, and I found myself driving around with friends and family, getting lost in bad neighborhoods and ultimately buying food, clothes, school supplies, and toys for children on the streets. I loved their laughter and the love they gave to us. We loved them in return! But there were so many and not enough hours in the day to help everyone.

After three years of visiting, someone suggested we coordinate our donations through the church and a local orphanage run by Fonicris, a foundation for disadvantaged and orphaned children. We began supporting the local orphanages most in need.

One sunny day, Henry brought our friend, the recording artist Marc Anthony, to the boy's home. It was a day that was written in the stars, when two influential powerhouses would take the project forward. Their support opened the door for dozens of projects that have touched more than 10,0000 children to date, from all walks of life, living with every challenge imaginable.

Five years later, we built a home that holds more than 100 boys. We obtained sponsors and mentors. We provide food, education, and a chance for a better future. Our efforts now include multiple housing projects in Dominican Republic, Colombia, Puerto Rico, Mexico, Colombia, Chile and Guatemala, with educational projects in Peru, Salvador, Bolivia and many more. Maestro Cares will soon complete its 13th project in Chicago.

The joy of giving is incomparable. I invite everyone to live life through compassion and the joy that giving awakens within you. Currently, I am a passionate, active board member of Maestro Cares, headquartered at Cardenas Marketing Network (CMN), the education agency where I have dedicated nearly 22 years of service working in music marketing, sponsorship, and branded entertainment through music and the arts.

I have encountered amazing mentors like Henry. I couldn't have asked for a better partner in love or better family and friends. Because I do not typically dwell on the past, this is the first time I have ever put it in writing. However, my mother, my sister, and Henry have taught me that no matter how tough things get, they could be much worse. This needs to be shared with the world.

I am always looking forward to the positive and exciting things that are coming my way. It's important to be grateful at all times and live every day giving. You will receive so much more in return!

REFLECTION

1. Who is the model for self-sacrifice in your life?
2. Do you look forward to the future with fear, curiosity, or excitement?
3. Who do you take care of? Is there still time to take care of you?

BIOGRAPHY

Elena Sotomayor is a Senior Level Branded Entertainment and Marketing Executive with demonstrated leadership skills, proven success in strategic ideation and innovation practices with a proven track record for orchestrating and activating sponsorships on national entertainment programs for Fortune 500 brands. She is a leader in innovative thinking with the ability to quickly recognize growth and unique marketing opportunities within the entertainment, experiential, and branded content marketing space. She has 14 years of experience in experiential marketing and event marketing platforms.

Recognized as an entrepreneurial think tank with the ability to direct and oversee various national initiatives around the country for her clients, Elena also works as Brand and Client Concierge within her company, Cardenas Marketing Network (CMN), managing top-level relationships and extensive marketing platforms from the ground up. Her strength lies in bringing plans to life and building ideation platforms with global brands such as Wrigley, Bud Light, Sprint, U.S Army, Burger King, Chevy and Johnson & Johnson.

Elena melds her passion for entrepreneurship and philanthropy as a board member with Maestro Cares, a foundation which builds orphanages to provide Latin American children with healthy and safe environments to support their academic dreams and basic every day needs.

Elena Sotomayor
elena@cmnevents.com
maestrocares.org
#sotomayorelena
(773) 908-9548

CREATE YOUR OWN DESTINY

Keila González Báez

"While you think about it, you are not doing it."

It was January of 2010. I was 26 years old and had an idea that had been rolling around in my head, trapped inside of me for months: I wanted to create my own magazine. I had recently left a media company where I had worked without pay for several months. It was there that the idea took shape.

At the media company, I had access to many valuable resources and held many positions. I was a copywriter, saleswoman, debt collector and public relations officer. Anything they asked me to do, I did. I was not even reimbursed for the public transportation to my job, but I learned everything I needed to know about publishing a magazine.

Even though I was very young, I realized that many times I was the one who was directing my boss, not the other way around. It made me understand that it was time to leave and do things on my own. So I retired from that publishing company and spent a few months giving shape to my dream. I swore to myself that I would never work for anyone from 8-6 every day, even if I had to starve.

A few months went by and at the same time I was trapped

in a toxic relationship. I was the victim of an abusive man who abused me for the most illogical things, like smiling or having a conversation with someone of the opposite sex. One time, someone stole my car and he gave ME a severe beating. It was crazy!

But the day came when I had had enough.

TERROR AND EPIPHANY

That day, I remember being kicked down the stairs of the common corridor of the apartment where we lived, and then having to climb each step back up with him pulling my long hair, again and again. There was no way out (at least I thought) until I heard a metallic sound that I will never forget. It was a knife that came rolling towards me on the floor. Then I heard the voice of his brother, with whom we lived (and who would die of an overdose several months later).

"Kill that bitch to shut up!" he said.

Then I realized the moment was literally life or death. I thought I was going to be stabbed to death. So without knowing where my strength came from (perhaps adrenaline?), my survival instinct woke up and I was able to miraculously escape from him.

I ran without looking back, trying to clean the blood mixed with tears that fell uncontrollably down my face. Finally, I collapsed on the edge of the street, receiving the rays of sunshine. At that moment, I felt the desire to do something really great and powerful to help others live a happier, more fulfilled life. It's a mission that still guides my company, Bienetre Media Group, today.

As with most ventures, the beginning wasn't easy. When I escaped from my near death situation, I didn't look back. I left behind clothes and my cell phone, but I was full of hope and I held on to it to keep going every day no matter what happened. It was madness that a person like me, who did not even know where I was going to sleep, could be thinking about creating a magazine that would promote love and well-being in humanity. But I was determined to publish something to help people live a happier and healthier life through better food and lifestyle choices. This is how *Bienetre Magazine* was born.

A friend who knew my plans and my precarious situation told me, "You have to be crazy, thinking about a well-being magazine when you do not even have a place to sleep or anything to eat." But as I have always said, start with what you have, not with what you need. I started with what I had at that time, and I set out to create the appropriate conditions for my entrepreneurship to flourish. At that point, I only had pencil, paper, good intentions and a purpose.

FORWARD, NO MATTER WHAT

I managed to move the project forward even though I was homeless and slept practically anywhere I could. A cousin gave me some clothes and welcomed me into her house during the first week; after that, I had to sleep at the homes of friends, relatives, and even new friends.

I still had family but they lived miles away and I couldn't bear to return to them, ten years later, empty-handed. But this was not going to stop me from achieving my goal. *If I have survived to this point, it must be for something*, I said to myself, *so let's make it worthwhile.*

I had always thought that all you need is a computer, a smart phone and an internet connection to start a business. However, in my experience I would say you don't even need that! The first proposals I sent to potential clients I created at an internet center for $30 an hour. I made calls to customers from a public phone and always used the same one so they believed it was my mobile phone. Imagine the impression you would make on a client if you called him from a different number each time!

My point here is simple. Stephen Dolley used to say, "One who wants to do something will find a way. One who doesn't, will find an excuse." Thank God I heard that one day and it has ruled my life since. I hope it helps you too if you're really determined to achieve success in whatever you set out to do.

The days passed and I was gaining more and more customers, thanks to the reputation I had built when I worked at the magazine. If I told a customer I was going to get something done, I would not beat around the bush or make excuses. I used honesty, perseverance and credibility to help me earn my customer's trust and build the business that will soon celebrate a decade of success.

A PLAN FOR DESTINY

I believe every woman can create her own destiny. Here are some things I have learned that may help you on your journey.

1. **Learning is more important than education.** I do not have a bachelor's or master's degree from any university. However, not a day goes by that I don't learn something. I think being an entrepreneur is a career, like law or medicine. You should always stay current in your profession, but for that you do not need a big title or degree, just a desire to learn. If you must have a degree to succeed, Mark Zuckerberg and Steve Jobs would not have dropped out of college. Degrees and titles are not necessary, but education is. So look on the internet, read books and ask people who are more advanced than you to recommend resources to help you move forward on your path to success.

2. **Have a Growth Attitude.** You must train your mind every day to grow and change. Stretch yourself by looking for new things, taking a risk, meditating, emulating more successful people, etc. It's the only way you can learn and grow.

3. **Lead, don't supervise.** One of the most important things I have learned is to surround myself with awesome people who give their all to accompany me in building my dream. Without them, I am nothing in my company. Learn to see your collaborators as collaborators, not employees. I do not even use the term

"employee" for people who help me build my business every day. I do not think of myself as doing them a favor to pay them for what they do; on the contrary, I am grateful that they dedicate their time and energy to make our company an extraordinary organization.

4. **Decide, don't delay.** I believe that while you think about it, you are not doing it. That means if you think about something too much, you will end up doing nothing or doing it halfway. Most people miss the opportunity to do something great because they are thinking about it. I am one who decides quickly, and if something goes wrong along the way, I have the integrity and responsibility to fix it or take care of it. No one is going to kill you for making a mistake, so why worry?

5. **Be open to change and innovation.** Unlike most entrepreneurs, I do not fear change and I think this leads to opportunities. I believe if you fear little, you gain a lot. I'm not saying I never get scared; I'm just saying that the amount of fear that I give myself permission to feel is not enough to paralyze me. I invite you to take a risk. It does not matter if it's something unknown. Just try it. The best things sometimes come from the unfamiliar. Dare to innovate, dabble in new things, change procedures, products, services, etc. And after you do it, always expect the best. The vast majority

of human beings believe that things are going to go wrong. Change the pattern of thought away from the negative, and you will see that when you expect the best, 98 percent of the time you will get the best.

6. **Sometimes you have to let go.** Two years after I launched my magazine, I had the opportunity to have my own radio show. I took the chance, because as you know, I'm an innovator. But what I did not understand at 27 years of age was that sometimes things don't work and letting go of them is not a bad thing. While I do believe in persevering, I now realize that it is not always the answer.

I held on to the radio show for three years until I transitioned it to a podcast format and finally left that as well. At that time, I felt terrible, but even harder to face was the fact that during those years, I never earned a penny. All I did was take money from the magazine to support the radio program. In most cases, persistence is vital to achieve what you want, however, there are moments that you have to let go for the sake of your physical, mental, and even financial health.

If you ask me how to know when to persevere and when to let go, I would say pay attention to how it makes you feel as you are trying to decide. If every time you do something it feels uncomfortable, gives you a headache, drains you of your strength and leaves you mentally depleted, you probably should let it go. If on the other hand, despite being exhausted, you feel something that drives you to continue and gives you joy, then it's time to continue.

And finally, recognize failure as a possibility, not the end of the world. After all, if you are going to fail, it is difficult for you to anticipate or avoid it (even if you are giving 100 percent). Only by failing will you be able to plan and execute it better next time.

Because my first company is led by people who make my life easier and allow me to continue expanding my creativity and entrepreneurship, I am now leading a second company that I have named "Author in 90 Days," where I teach others to write and sell their books. So if you are in a situation like I was, always remember that there is a light at the end of the tunnel. You must take care of yourself and constantly grow. Gratitude is your best weapon and if you expect the best, you will receive the best.

REFLECTION

1. Have you ever had a near death experience? How did you react?

2. What do you think you absolutely need to be successful?

3. Do you always expect the best? Why or why not?

BIOGRAPHY

Keila González Báez has been an avid reader since she was a child and a writer since she was eight years old. Currently, she is the author of five books, three of them published and awarded as bestsellers. She is also founder and CEO of Bienetre Media Group, a publishing company that she founded at the age of 26.

During the last year, she has dedicated herself to helping others fulfill their dream of being an author through the "Author in 90 Days" program, which has already helped almost a dozen people successfully write, publish, and sell their books.

Keila has interviewed many celebrities for *Bientre* including Gloria Estefan, María Elena Salinas, Isabel Allende, and Dr. Ana María Polo. She has been recognized by the vice president of the Dominican Republic as an outstanding entrepreneur mother. She is often invited to appear as a voice for entrepreneurs in her country alongside billionaires and government leaders in national panel discussions and presentations. Keila is a single mother of a 13-year-old son whose father died when he was seven years old.

Keila González Báez
keilagonzalez.com
@keilagonzalezbaez
(809) 434-3135

THE ACCIDENTAL ADVOCATE

Ivonne Enid Hanks

"The Divine manifests itself through synchronized,
miraculous moments."

If anyone told me that I would someday become a community advocate, I would have looked at them with surprised disbelief, and responded with…eh? What!? Really?! Yet I actually did become an advocate and it was totally the doing of "Divine Grace Consciousness."

I grew up in a time and culture where protecting a girl's virginity for the sake of family honor was more important than the promise of her future. So I followed the cultural norm, married young, and became a non-traditional student, living an extraordinary life against all odds!

By the time I was 16 years old, I was a child bride. At 17, I was a teenage mother and a freshman in college. While my peers were enjoying the normal activities of high school, I was tackling child rearing, homemaking and household management duties while cramming in homework, exams, and term papers. Talk about experiencing a trifecta of life altering events!

As a child, I got along well with everyone, from the young to the old. The other kids would come to me and complain whenever anything went wrong because I am the type of person that expresses disapproval in the face of injustice. On many of the road trips to visit family in the countryside, one of the highlights for me was bringing the neediest children small gifts. I would share everything I had like toys, clothes, and candy.

Unbeknownst to me, my altruistic nature and childlike joy came from a state of being one with the flow. I can vividly recall the joy bursting from my heart to see others happy.

As much as I enjoyed hanging out with my peers, I equally loved spending time with the neighborhood elders, conversing about subjects I was curious about. I would hold "debates" with my father's amigos, always advocating for the equal status of girls and boys when it came to household chores. Back then, chores were culturally gender specific and girls were at a disadvantage.

They would tell my father, "Pedro, you've got your hands full!" Back then, girls were not supposed to speak out, but secretly my father reveled in the fact that I could hold my own.

THE GIFT OF DISCERNMENT: INTUITION

If I were to look back and identify the precise moment I became an advocate, it would be when I was a young child. Even when I wasn't aware of it, the flow lived within me.

When I was in seventh grade, there was a kid named Nogue who was the bully of the school. I was fortunate that for most of seventh grade, I didn't exist for Nogue, or, at least I had not come into his line of vision. But then came the day….

During a change of class periods, students were walking

single file down the hall one way while other students were passing from the opposite direction. As I glanced at the other passing faces, for a fraction of a second my eyes met Nogue's. Talk about divine timing!

I recall the feeling that I had. I knew that Nogue had just become aware of me, and it was not a "good feeling." As I passed him, I saw out of the corner of my eye that Nogue had reached for his mouth and pulled his bubblegum out. Then he swung his arm in my direction to glue the bubble gum into my hair.

At that precise moment, I spun around to fend off Nogue's swat at me with my left arm, which was healing from a broken wrist, and was in a cast. "Leave me alone!" I yelled. Noque slunk away, holding his arm.

The commotion that ensued was pure chaos! "Ivonne beat up Nogue!" I became the instant heroine!

This incident marked the moment I became aware of intuition. I had a sense of knowing, even though I could not consciously articulate it. So if you asked me today, I would respond with certainty that what I didn't know then is that I had trusted my intuition! I paid attention to that "unknowing knowing", *un yo no sé qué*, that somehow felt right. This "feeling" became my guiding compass through my life journey.

CONSCIOUSNESS: THE SOURCE OF AN ALTRUISTIC NATURE

After transitioning from marriage to single parenting, I relocated to New York. Upon my arrival, I secured a part-time job with the local medical college. I immediately enrolled in the local state university and focused on completing my studies.

At the time, I had a part-time income, unemployment benefits, and child support but it was not enough to cover expenses. I was referred to a child care subsidy assistance program at the Local Department of Social Services (LDSS). One of the eligibility requirements was to demonstrate proof of weekly earnings.

Every Friday, I would go to the LDSS to turn in a copy of my earnings. While seated in the disorderly waiting area, I would observe the people's personalities and feel the negatively charged atmosphere there. Most of all, I noticed the demeanor of the staff with the clientele. It was very rude and intimidating.

The staff were always complaining, resenting the clients, talking about how they hated their job, about their personal life in general, and being antagonistic towards the clients.

I was anxious whenever I approached the window. Back then, I didn't know English well. I enunciated differently than other people and the staff would mock my accent while encouraging other co-workers to join the "fun"...an abusive conduct that is known today as bullying.

Bullying was typical in many local health and human services agencies at that time. The incivility stemmed from an ill-conceived, collective notion that people receiving government assistance were asking for handouts and therefore were not worthy of respect.

ANGELS IN DISGUISE

I believe that the Divine manifests itself in all kind of shape and forms; it's an omnipresence that is everywhere. Like my mother used to say when we were kids, "Behave everywhere you go. You never know who is watching." Indeed, when I was dealing with those challenges in the LDSS, unbeknownst to me, somebody was watching.

One day, as I was leaving, one of the security guards ran after me and began to ask me all kind of questions. "Hey, where are you from? You speak Spanish, right? What brought you here?" At first, I was taken aback by the questions but my new friend, Mr. Jeffrey Gardner, asked me to follow him down the hall.

He stopped in front of a bulletin board, took down a post and handed it to me. He said, "I know this lady that comes here, and helps the Spanish-speaking people. You should give her a call. They are looking for people." Upon reading it, I learned that Catholic Charities of the Albany Dioceses, Hispanic Outreach Services was looking for a case manager.

There are no coincidences. Nothing happens by chance. These little miraculous moments are synchronicities and the manifestation of the Divine Consciousness leading one to their purpose.

Over the next few weeks, Mr. Gardner would ask me, "Did you call the lady?"

"I will. I will," I replied, but I kept postponing it. One day, he said, "I see how you handle the staff at the counter. I think you will be great for the job. I've seen you helping people here. You might as well get paid for it."

I responded that I did not meet the qualifications. They were looking for a candidate with a social work degree. I was a biology major.

"You already have what you need to do this job…you are already doing it!" he insisted.

A month later, I began working as a case manager. I had no idea what a case manager did. I even asked about it during the interview. That should have been enough for the Executive Director, Sister Anne Tranelli, to put my resume away. But of course not! Who am I to question Divine's order?

THE EMERGING OF A MINDFUL LEADER

Once I accepted the job, everything went smoothly. It was a full-time position and the classes I needed to complete my degree were available at t at Russell Sage Colleges at night. All this happened within a matter of weeks, from mid-May to September. I finished the semester at SUNY in May, and by September, I transferred to Russell Sage and started night classes.

My first assignment as a case manager was to assist the LDSS with the Spanish-speaking population. Talk about a reversal of roles! This time, I was approaching the window as an advocate, not as a client.

The reaction of the staff, upon learning that I was the new case manager, was priceless! They liked that I was there to assist the clientele with translations, however, they also joked that I was responsible for bringing more clientele. "Did we just get a *@#%* busload dumped on us?" they would ask. "Where do you keep finding these people?!" They kept calling the clientele "these people." Geez!

Through these experiences, I realized that the challenges with the customer relations in the health and human service agencies was due to a lack of cultural intelligence and ability to successfully conduct business across cultural barriers. I provided the support to bridge this gap when I was hired in 1997 to work at the LDSS.

My job was to man the front desk providing translation and interpretation to the clientele. A couple of years later, I transitioned to work with the state. Talk about coincidences! No such thing…

In 2010, I answered to a call to action to become a Commissioner of Human Rights for the City of Albany—both literally and figuratively. The call came from an established community leader that asked if I would apply for the position. We proceeded to have the same kind of conversation I did with Mr. Gardner ten years earlier.

"They are not going to call me," I said. "They are not too fond of advocates."

"Well, you should apply anyway. They claim they don't have that many minorities applying because they can't find talent in the community. We need to demonstrate otherwise. Please apply. Send your resume. You've got nothing to lose."

Next thing I knew, I was on the Commission. Heed, child, heed the Divine!

During my tenure with the Human Rights Commission

I found that it was more of a political group trying to look good than an action group doing the work the community so desperately needed.

I actively began to advocate for the need for proactive outreach by promoting cultural strategies that would encourage tolerance and inclusion within the communities. However, the lack of vision, cultural intelligence and mindfulness in the leadership was limited and obstructive. I understood then that in places where light gathers to do the work of the collective good, there will also be the opposite energy.

Community advocacy and politics are not for the faint of heart. It takes presence and heart to advocate for the common good of the collective. I became a community advocate because I heeded and trusted Divine's Guidance purpose for me.

Today I know with certainty that there are no coincidences in life. Nothing happens by chance. The Divine manifests through synchronized, miraculous moments. When we are in a state of presence, being one with the flow, we are in the best state to recognize and act on these synchronicities to co-create our intentions aligned with the Divine Consciousness' purpose for us.

Every single one of us is an expression of the Divine in the human condition. We are endowed with innate gifts and talents to manifest and share with the world.

The only requisite: you must be willing to live a life from a beautiful state of being fully present and engaged in life. Breathe deep; be here now. Dream big, rise, and play full out!

REFLECTION

1. Are you aware that coincidences are synchronized, little miracles from the Divine, God?

2. Do you ever heed your Divine's guidance? Do you listen to your intuition?

3. Would you speak up if you saw an inhumane, uncivil act against another or others? Do you engage in civic participation?

BIOGRAPHY

Ivonne Hanks is passionate about the ability that lies in every individual and believes that everyone can find their way to a more balanced existence, as well as make a difference in their civic engagement. She has had a lengthy career in public service within the health and human services field. She holds advanced degrees in the fields of political science and public health.

She is President of Health is You, LLC an integrative transformative health and wellness strategist practice which coaches and helps individuals and families find balance in a heart-centered, purpose-driven life. Ivonne is also the President of Worldwide Culture-Link, LLC, an innovative and strategic communications consulting firm in social marketing, cultural intelligence, and mindful leadership.

Ivonne became the first Latina to be appointed as a Commissioner to the City of Albany, New York Human Rights Commission. She has been featured as a speaker/panelist for New York State Assembly's Puerto Rican Hispanic Task Force SOMOS Conference, providing cultural intelligence expertise. Today, Ivonne offers a wide range of transformative and mindful leadership strategies and interventions from individual and group coaching to seminars, and guest speaking appearances.

Ivonne Enid Hanks
healthwellnessmuse@gmail.com
(518) 424-9930

Maria Castro

"Building a Better Tomorrow for Everyone, Today."

We are all the creators of our own masterpiece made from the many colors and brush strokes called life. Each of our ancestors have woven a piece of our story like a tapestry unique to every one of us. And we continue to create ours for our children and grandchildren.

My story, like many in this book, is filled with amazing people that have brought me to where I am today. I recently received my DNA results and it didn't surprise me. I'm 60 percent Native American, 18 percent Spaniard, 11 percent French and three percent Portuguese, with sprinkles of many other ethnicities.

A WONDERFUL PAST

I am descended from a long line of proud Texans who were most likely Native American Indians who settled in the southern part of the state. My dad, Jose Reyes Maltos, was born in Crystal City, Texas and raised there by his siblings and uncles due to the untimely death of both of his parents (Jose Maltos and Santos Trevino Reyes). My mother, Maria Oralia Cuevas-Maltos, was born in Dilley, Texas and raised in Crystal City, Texas where she met my dad.

The 1930's were not kind to people of color in south Texas, so communities and schools were segregated. My parents met in elementary school and made their First Holy Communion together, then fell in love in high school and got married. They had four children: Jose Luis, Alma Delia, Dora Alicia and me, Maria Oralia.

My dad, like many other Mexicans in Texas, was a migrant worker and travelled from city to city with my mom and brother in tow. It was a hard life for them and my dad wanted to provide more for his growing family. He became a printer apprentice and eventually, a full-fledged printer and moved our family to Chicago in hope of finding work. He worked two jobs for many years until he became an entrepreneur and opened his own printing business.

We lived on Cullerton Street in Chicago's Pilsen community and the printing business was located in our basement. His business flourished in the mid 1970's and he had clients from all over the Chicago area as well as Michigan and Wisconsin. He printed posters, invitations, raffle tickets, flyers, and menus. Initially the name of the print shop was Imprenta Maltos but was changed to J&O Printing, which stood for Jose and Oralia. My mom was his partner and it was only fair that the name change included both owners.

My mother, a homemaker, was creative and resourceful with the family budget. She managed to keep us all in private school, extracurricular activities, and dressed very nicely due to her amazing talent as a seamstress. She had hot meals for us daily and never complained when any of us brought over a friend for some of her excellent cooking, all while running the office and finances as well as the linotype machine.

On any given day I would come home and hear music playing as my father whistled and worked. Most days when I arrived home from school, I would grab him and dance with him. We were very blessed to have such hardworking parents who provided so well for us. I owe a debt of gratitude to them both for the life I was privileged to have.

My parents were married for over 50 years before my dad's passing on April 19, 2002. My dad was a romantic at heart and would often surprise my mother with trips, serenading her with mariachi music for her birthday, and holding hands everywhere they went. We are blessed to still have my mother. She still spoils us with her homemade cooking, love, and advice. Like my parents, I married my high school sweetheart, Martin Castro. Today, 42 years later, the love and bond we share is unbreakable. I am blessed to call him my husband, friend, lover, co-pilot, and most of all my biggest supporter.

JOYFUL ROAD TRIPS

We travelled frequently to San Antonio, Texas to see our maternal grandparents, (Margarito Cuevas and Guadalupe Camero-Cuevas), uncles, aunts, and cousins. It was always an adventure.

My earliest memories were of us piling in the car with our luggage on top, fresh *taquitos de chorizo y huevos* (sausage & eggs), *papas con huevos* (potatoes and eggs) and plenty of snacks. It was a long drive, so we had comic books, dolls, and road games to entertain us along the way. We played Slug Bug by punching each other when we were the first to spot a VW Beetle passing by. There were also many stops at the Native American depots to purchase our favorite moccasins.

Anticipation of arriving at our grandparent's house was too much to bear at times. We would calculate the miles left before we arrived or until we could jump out and stretch our legs. It seemed like we always reached our grandparent's house in the middle of the night, but my grandparents were always waiting up and excited to see us.

The next morning, we would wake to the smell of fresh, homemade flour tortillas, *chorizo con huevos, papitas fritas* (fried potatoes) and *frijoles* (beans). Our cousins lived a few blocks away and were always happy to see us. My brother would entertain us by playing his guitar and singing songs for us to pass the time. At night we would hang out until it was time for bed and my grandpa would spread out blankets and have us all lay down on the grass and say a prayer: "I see the moon and the moon sees me; God bless the moon and God bless me." Now I continue the tradition with my grandchildren to keep his memory alive.

We would spend a few days in San Antonio before heading out to Crystal City to visit our Reyes-Maltos relatives. My tio Victor Maltos owned a small grocery store and we could not contain our excitement, knowing we would get all the Coca-Cola, chips, and candy we wanted once we arrived. Crystal

City is known as the city of Popeye because it was once filled with acres of spinach. Today, they still celebrate with an annual Popeye festival which brings lots of former residents back for the festivities. I have fond memories of our trips and love going back to visit whenever I get the chance.

BUILDING A BETTER TOMORROW FOR EVERYONE, TODAY

As I reflect on the many jobs I have held throughout my career, I see that they taught me many lessons about doing what you love to do. Early on, I worked in the radio industry representing Spanish radio at a time when advertising agencies were not including Hispanics in their local market media buys. We had to work ten times harder than our general market counterparts for the few dollars budgeted for Spanish radio. I managed to do well anyway because of my persistence and overall talent for sales, but it wasn't easy.

Later, as I entered the field of retail marketing, I found a real sense of creativity in producing events for consumers locally and then nationally for multiple shopping centers. The buying power of Hispanics was really picking up steam and I took full advantage of it by promoting goods to both general and Hispanic consumers. I then continued work in event marketing and production for two national companies that represented such clients as Proctor & Gamble, American Express, Kraft, Nestle and many others. Producing events in predominately Hispanic markets was all the rage and companies were seeing the return on their investments and clamoring to get their market share. Today, I am proud to say that I work for one of the most socially responsible communications companies around: Comcast. They don't just talk the talk; they walk the walk.

Our secret sauce? Servant leadership and helping to improve the lives of so many people in the communities where we work, live, and play.

I have been able to bring resources back to Pilsen, the community where I was born and raised, as well as to many other amazing nonprofits who each provide unique and much needed services to better the lives of people in underserved communities. Comcast provides scholarships, grants, and thousands of hours of volunteering all year round. And that is what I consider building a better tomorrow for everyone, today!

Comcast also encourages us to lend our time and talents to local nonprofits we are passionate about and I currently serve on the Women's Business Development Center Advisory Council, Hispanic Scholarship Fund Chicago Council and the Telemundo Chicago Community Action Board. I believe if you don't have a seat at the table, you have to bring your own chair.

CHALLENGES AND OPPORTUNITIES

Challenges are opportunities in disguise. Life has its way of causing disruptions no matter who you are or where you come from. Like many, I have had my share of extreme loss and disappointment, starting with the loss of my grandparents, who I loved very deeply.

My second loss was the most profound--my father. He had a personality the size of Texas. He loved his family more than anything in this world. He was an amazing provider, a lover of music, great food, traveling and holidays (especially Christmas). He was a strict disciplinarian but had a heart of gold. There wasn't anything he wouldn't do for us. When I lost him, it shattered my world into a million pieces. The hole in my heart was too much to bear at times.

But then came the birth of our first granddaughter, Savannah Christine Castro, in October of 2003. Life was grand again and the opportunity to shower her with love was just the healing I needed. Then came the birth of my one and only grandson, Martin Joseph Castro V (MJ), on Christmas 2005. Being surrounded by their unconditional love was perfect and just what the doctor ordered. But on June 4, 2012, I was devastated to lose my daughter-in-law and mother of my grandchildren, Renee Guerrero-Castro.

Nothing could have prepared us for that. How do you explain to two young children that their mommy is never coming home? It wasn't easy. Right before her passing she said to me, "My kids are going to be okay; you and pop have always taken good care of them and I know they will be just fine." It gave me comfort to know that she felt at peace before leaving this earth. Her untimely death taught me so much. The phrase "Tomorrow is promised to none of us," really resonated with me.

We knew we all had to work to put the pieces back together as best we could, and we did. As a family, we have helped our son raise his children and it has been one of our greatest joys. It's been challenging at times, but always rewarding at the end of each day.

Today, Savannah and MJ are 15 and 13 and still a big part of our daily lives. They now have two new baby sisters, Amaya Sofia (3 years old), Aaliyah Marie (four months old) and a new bonus mom, Jessica, who they love very much. Today, I continue to face what I think are insurmountable challenges at times, but as I reflect on my faith, I know that God is with me every step of the way.

THINGS I AM MOST PROUD TO BE

I am proud to be the daughter of Jose and Oralia Maltos; the wife of the love of my life, Martin Castro; the mother of Martin and Phillip Castro and the grandmother of Savannah, MJ, Amaya and Aaliyah Castro; the mother-in-law of Jessica Rys-Castro and Jessica Montoya-Castro; a sister to Joe, Alma and Dora; a friend to many incredible people; a sassy, kind, daring, Latina over 60 years old; a Leo; adventurous, passionate, resilient and able to take a seat at the table; and someone who inspired the declaration of Maria Castro Day in the City of Aurora.

REFLECTION

1. How has your past shaped your present?
2. Do you view challenges as obstacles or opportunities?
3. What are you most proud to be?

BIOGRAPHY

For 30 years, Maria has worked extensively in three sectors: retail, consumer packaged goods, and telecommunications. She joined Comcast in 2005, where she helps implement and manage programs that deliver social and business value to nonprofit organizations and communities. Comcast is known for achieving social impact through innovative employee engagement, solid community partnerships, and CSR initiatives like grants, scholarships, volunteer opportunities, and event sponsorships of local community events.

As part of the Comcast community investment team, Maria identifies corporate giving opportunities for Comcast's core focus areas of youth leadership, volunteerism, digital literacy and work force development. Born and raised in the Pilsen community, she has brought many needed resources there and to other Chicago area nonprofits as well. What's the recipe to her secret sauce you ask? Resilience, compassion, kindness, love of family and friends, volunteerism, honesty, trailblazing, and happiness.

She currently serves as the Chairwoman for the Hispanic Scholarship Fund's Chicago Council, Telemundo Chicago Community Action Board, and the Women's Business Development Center's Advisory Council. Maria resides in Riverside and has been married to her husband, Martin, for 42 years. They have two sons, Marty Jr. and Phil, two daughter-in-laws named Jessica and four grandchildren: Savannah, MJ, Amaya and Aaliyah.

Maria Castro
Instagram: maria_castro803
Twitter: @castromaria803

Veronica Antunez

"Love yourself so much that you can empty yourself in others."

From the ground up, everything looks overwhelming. That's why you have to stand up, face what's in front of you, and dream of something even greater.

One day I was out to eat with my two daughters and they asked me to tell them about my life before they were born. After all, they had three older stepsisters and they knew I had been married before. After I told them my story, my older daughter encouraged me to share it. She said she thought other women could be inspired to believe that they can do great things by themselves. My friend, Gloria Romo (who appeared in Volume IV) thought the same thing, so I said to myself, *let's do it, Veronica!* So here I am.

I do believe that the people and events that we have in our lives can either help us to or take us away from our ability to dream and love ourselves. If you make mistakes, it's important to see your mistakes as life lessons and regard them with love. Life is nothing without love, and love is the flame that symbolizes the higher life that I call "God of Light."

Since I saw the light, I am unstoppable, powerful and

confident. I have learned that I always win with the experiences that life gives me or I win when I learn more. It's as simple as that. You must learn to live because the world is full of living people who are dead, and the cemeteries are full of dead people who never lived! Every day is a new life to live!

Love the light that guides you with wisdom because where there is love, everything good becomes eternal. Love is the secret to everything. And it is most important to love yourself. Love yourself so much that you can empty yourself in others!

LESSONS OF YOUTH

I was born in Mexico and moved to a small town in the center of the Mexican Republic when I was nine years old. We lived well, in a big house with all the comforts anyone would want. I even attended private school. I would say that my childhood was happy in every way except for my father's absence.

He owned a business in Mexico City and remained there to work most of the time. He was never with us for important dates like Father's Day, Christmas, or even my graduation. On that day, I pretended he was in the audience, smiling and proud of me. I always wished he had spent more time with us and didn't understand why he could not since he was the boss and could take off whenever he wanted. To my young mind, it seemed like if he wanted to be with us, he would be. Truly, no amount of money can buy the absence of a father.

My mother is very special. She tried to educate my sisters and me in the best way possible. She taught us moral principles that are rooted deep within me. My mother is very conservative, and we often see life in different ways, but I love her with all my soul.

We spent Christmas holidays at the home of my great grandparents. My great grandmother (we called her Mom Nena) always woke us up early to open the presents that Santa Claus brought, and she would play with us. I still remember Mom Nena's eyes full of love for us. I still miss her and love her very much.

In the summer of 1987, I married a man seven years older than me even though I was still a teenager. I was studying accounting and wanted to become a public accountant. However, I was unaware that the man I married was actually a violent, typical, macho, Mexican male.

For 12 years I suffered from physical and mental domestic violence. He was controlling and made me end my friendships with others. Luckily, he worked in Chicago, and only stayed in Mexico for one or two months a year, but those times seemed like an eternity.

I did not say anything to my family because my mother was against divorce. She was also worried about what people were going to say, and we had three daughters to consider. I was careful not to talk to my daughters negatively about their father. Since I did not have friends anymore, I sunk into a depression. Everything seemed overwhelming and I wondered how I could endure any more.

NEW HOPE

Everything began to change when I went to a three-day spiritual retreat. There, I discovered myself and I realized that I was strong and could do many things. First and foremost, I could say NO! I thought this one simple word could change everything.

My marital situation was still difficult, but I was not afraid of my husband anymore. Instead, I confronted him. I went to the police station to file a report against him with the Mexican police. I told them he had physically hurt me, and I showed them the medical test results to support my accusation. However, they did nothing. He was not prosecuted. Unfortunately, my family did not support me in my actions against him either.

Three months later, he asked me to go live with him in the United States and start a new life. I accepted right away because I saw the opportunity to end my misery. I know that the laws in the U.S. against domestic violence were better, and I saw my salvation ahead.

We arrived in Chicago in August 2001. I loved my new city and a few days later, I started working in an office doing telemarketing. Unfortunately, my husband had not changed. He still treated me badly, but he did not dare beat me. Still, I was constantly on guard for my children. As their mother, it was my duty to protect them. We felt the need to call the police only once, but when they arrived, my three little girls were so upset and crying, they broke my heart. They begged me not to let them take their father away and I couldn't bring myself to let him be arrested. Things were better then, and they were about to get even better.

A FRESH START

We had been living in Chicago for about two years when the unimaginable happened. One day, while I was at work, he left the house and never came back. Apparently, he went to live in Oklahoma City and we have not heard from him since. His departure was a great help in securing a divorce, which I sought right away.

When I went to court with my lawyer, I was nervous, and my stomach was filled with butterflies. But when I walked out of the courtroom, I felt an indescribable happiness that can only come from experiencing true, beautiful freedom. The day was suddenly different. In only three months from the time he left, the divorce was finalized, he was legally out of our life, and my girls and I finally felt safe. It was as if we had been given a fresh start to make our way in the world!

Soon after, I met a man who was the exact opposite of my first husband. Juan Antunez and I first met in Dunkin Donuts and we became fast friends. He was divorced too but had been granted custody of his three children. I knew he was a loving, kind, and stable man and he has been an angel in my life and to my three daughters as well.

In 2005, we married and blended our family of six. I love Juan's children and they love me too. they have thanked me many times for being their mom. We were all together for a very brief time though because our older children were soon out on their own.

Meanwhile, Juan and I added two daughters of our own to our special family. I am so grateful my girls have such a loving family and I am grateful to him for his love and support throughout the years. I am also grateful to my strong mother, who raised six girls almost completely on her own and had to celebrate so many Christmases and other holidays without our father. I admire her and thank her for showing me such a wonderful example of love.

So many women leave their country, their friends, and their family with the hope of building a better life. We leave behind the comfort of home to start from scratch and create a life that's full of hope and love, without fear. Today, I live well in my new country. I travel with my family several times a year, we do not have debts, and we feel that everything is possible when we always look forward.

Yesterday does not exist anymore; we only have today. However, we are always thinking that we will have a better tomorrow. Every day when we wake up, we are given new life. It is an opportunity to do things better than yesterday and when things get difficult, we have to be stronger because we have our children watching us and they want to be like us.

It is better to grow strong children than fix broken adults. Show them that everything is possible and if they tell you that they cannot do something, show them that the best things are worth the hard work. That's why very few people dare do them.

Fear is only in the mind. We must dominate the fear before the fear dominates us. Everything is possible; just take action and we can change the world!

Please don't forget that if you seek it, you will always find the light to leave where you are. If you do not see it, that means you are that light and you need to discover yourself. Always remember to value yourself, but above all, love yourself, as nobody else in the world loves you. You are a great woman and can withstand everything and stand against everyone. Believe in yourself as a powerful woman.

REFLECTION

1. Do you love yourself?
2. When is it hard for you to say "no?" What can you do to make it easier?
3. Who (or what) is the greatest light in your life?

BIOGRAPHY

Veronica Antunez was born and raised in Mexico where she graduated as a public accountant. She married and suffered years of domestic violence before coming to America, divorcing her husband, and receiving custody of her three daughters.

Veronica remarried Juan Artunez, a man who adopted her children as his own. Thanks to his love and support, they are now all self-sufficient professionals. Veronica and Juan's two youngest daughters keep them busy with ballet classes and violin lessons.

Veronica is a licensed loan officer, does telemarketing for her husband, and voiceover work for different internet companies. She and her husband are members of many marketing networks and currently have groups of people working in the U.S., Mexico, South America, parts of Europe, and the Philippines. This allows them to travel and work from wherever they are, taking pleasure in teaching and supporting people who want to learn.

She is also learning to play violin and continually improve her English.

She likes to tell people, "Believe in yourself and you will be unstoppable!"

Veronica (Unica) Antunez
veroantunez@gmail.com
(708) 979-1823

Leonor Gil

"Experiences will help you grow, learn, and become stronger."

It was a warm, balmy, summer night outside the house where I lived in my hometown of Uruapan, Michoacan. There I was, at the age of five, screaming at the top of my lungs, *"No, no te vayas, mama!"* (Mom, don't leave!), as she slowly and painfully peeled my fingers away away from her left arm and walked away!

All of a sudden, I felt like I couldn't breathe. My heart was pounding and hurting in my chest, and it felt very heavy. Did someone just punch my gut? I was still screaming and never knew my eyes could make so many tears. They streamed down my face for hours after she left. Every cell in my body was in shock. Little did I know that my life would change forever!

A ROCKY START

I am the third oldest of four children. Ever since I can remember, my mom worked hard for us to make ends meet and make sure my two older brothers and my younger sister and I had a roof over our head. My dad would disappear after each one of us was born. I knew him, but also knew he had another family. Later, after his passing in my teen years, I discovered he had several families who claimed him as their own. I ended up with 23 half brothers and sisters I never knew I had!

Before mom left, I was very happy and life was good. After her departure, my sister and I continued living with our grandmother, Abuelita Mariquita (who became my second mom), and my Uncle Jose (the only father-figure I have ever known), who was still in school. Then the day came when my grandmother got a call from my grandfather. The only "mother" my sister and I had ever known had to leave too.

This was the beginning of a five-year long, sad phase in my life. Over the next several years, we bounced around like ping-pong balls, from household to household. We ended up living with my aunt, my mom's younger sister, who had six children of her own and was squeezed for space and resources.

I never felt like I belonged there, even though they were family. We were treated differently than the cousins. I missed my mom dreadfully, especially at night when I cried myself to sleep with the excruciating pain of migraines. The holidays were the hardest. While everyone was happy, laughing, and enjoying the company of their families, I was experiencing a gut-wrenching, heart-crushing, punched-in-the-gut feeling as I missed my mom, Abuelita, and the father I hardly knew. Our only consolation was dear Uncle Jose. He was our defender, our savior and the one dear thing we could hold onto during this time. Thank you, Tio Jose, for being there for us when we needed you most!

In our fifth year, we moved in with a single mom with three older daughters. That year was the loneliest and most painful, as we experienced rejections, dismissals, negative comments, lack of love, contempt, resentment, jealousy, etc. to remind us we did not belong there. The single mom suffered from seizures and my sister and I were blamed for them!

The day finally came when my mom arrived to take us to Chicago with her. What a joyous day! After five long years of pain, suffering, and loneliness, I could finally hug and kiss my mom. She was so pretty, smelled so good, looked like a million bucks, and to some extent, seemed so strange to me. It still felt like she had abandoned me!

WELCOME TO CHICAGO

In the cold winter of 1974, my mom brought us to Chicago where we joined my grandparents. The journey to from Mexico to Chicago was an experience itself. Wearing a light white coat, pants, and thin socks, I can still feel my frozen toes inside my shoes. This was the start of a new life for me.

We arrived on January 31. The school year had started already, and mom could not get us into a school, so I spent days looking out the window at the cold weather. My siblings and I fought a lot during the day. In the "Little Village" neighborhood, we shared a one-bedroom apartment with my grandparents – a total of seven of us living in very close quarters. Every afternoon around five o'clock, as soon as the door to the tiny apartment opened and my mom walked in, my siblings and I flocked over her, each complaining about what the other had done and who was to blame. Looking back at those days now, my love and admiration for my mom grew stronger as I came to understand what it's like to come home after a long, hard day at work to find whining children!

I enrolled in school in the middle of seventh grade. That first semester was very difficult because not only did I not know the language, but we were teased and bullied by the other kids, especially the gang-affiliated girls.

Every single day my admiration, love, and concern for my mom grew stronger. I saw how hard she struggled to make ends meet and ensure we had what we needed. She never seemed to take time for herself but kept working and moving from job to job in search of better pay and better hours.

One day on my way to school, I remember thinking about how hard she worked in factories and restaurants. That day I knew I did not want to end up like my mom. I vowed to myself that I would have a better life. I would start by staying in school, even though I had considered quitting and working to help her instead. The following year in eighth grade, I was honored for learning English the fastest and made the honor roll! I went on to Kelly High School where I made the National Honor roll and graduated in the top ten of more than 300 students in my class. I made my mom very proud!

During my last year in high school, I met the man who would become my husband and the father to my two beautiful children, Carol and Jorge. When I was only 19, he proposed, and by age 20, I was married to him.

My husband had moved to Houston to find work a few

months before our wedding and the day after we wed, I moved to Houston with him. The next five years were extremely difficult as I had no family or friends in town and I was a full-time student at the University of Houston as well as a full-time wife!

Also, our marriage was becoming dysfunctional. We fought often, jealousy and verbal and physical abuse became the norm. I had started to make friends, but I still felt that my husband was the one and only person in my life, even though our relationship was not working.

One day, after we had fought about something, he said he was leaving me! Noooo, not again! I could not bear the thought of the only person I had in my life leaving me! I ran after him in tears and the feeling that followed was very familiar. There it was again, streams of tears down my cheeks, screaming at the top of my lungs…"DON'T GO PLEASE!" The all too familiar feeling of loneliness, heart-crushing pain, inability to breathe, and the punched-in-the-gut sensation were back. And he was gone, just like the day my mom left for Chicago!

The pain was too much to endure. I felt I had no one to call, to turn to, to ask for help. Life did not seem worth living. I frantically searched the bathroom cabinet for one of his razor blades and found one. It was the answer to my pain. I proceeded to slit my left wrist many times. I must have passed out because when I woke up, I was covered in blood but still alive. The pain was still there, but he was gone.

Somehow, with a lot of effort, I started cleaning up the bloody mess. I fell asleep, tired and weak from losing so much blood, and by dawn, he was back! I never told my family back in Chicago about this horrendous experience. Instead, I started to seek counseling for my abandonment issues while still in school.

Although my grades suffered, I graduated with a bachelor's degree in finance. I was so proud! I had made it and it was time to find a real job! Unfortunately, the economy was now in the middle of a recession. Finding a job in Houston was almost impossible and my husband and I decided to move back to Chicago.

We continued to struggle as a couple. I knew this was not the kind of life I wanted to live. But for some reason, I would not leave with the children. Then one day, during a fight, he threw me across the room and I landed on my rear. I could not get up from the floor. That was it! I had to break the cycle. I could not afford to have my children witness behavior I would never want them to model. But someone had to take the first step. So I gathered strength and filed for a divorce.

The divorce felt like the world was crumbling and I was going down with it! My faith in God, my mom, my family, and the love of my young children gave me the strength and adeptness to continue with life. I was finally freed of the shackles of abandonment. I knew I would be ok and that the children and I could go on with our lives. Now it was my time to be their sole provider, just as my mom had done for so many years. However, I had the privilege of being a successful, educated Latina, unlike my mom who had to work in a factory. God bless you, mom!

MY MOM, MY GREATEST GOD-GIVEN GIFT

In May of 2015, my mom was diagnosed with renal sarcoma. Over the years, no matter how many times she was poked or how much pain she endured, she never complained. She maintained her positive spirit and kept a beautiful smile on her face. She never wanted to worry her "beautiful daughters."

In October of 2018, the doctors gave mom approximately six months to live. At our Thanksgiving dinner a month later, I thanked her from the bottom of my heart for having made that enormous sacrifice to bring us to the U.S. for a better life and enduring sleepless nights without her children, cold days standing at the bus stop to get to work, endless criticism for abandoning her children, verbal abuse at workplaces, etc. I finally accepted that her departure was not abandonment but love for her children.

On December 5, my mom passed away. While her death brought back all those terrible feelings again, I knew she was not abandoning me. I know that while she is not with me in person, she will always be with me in spirit. Thanks to her, I have learned that what does not kill you only makes you stronger!

No matter what life throws at us, know that there is light and hope on the other side and experiences will help you grow, learn, and become stronger. I am grateful to my beautiful, extraordinary mom, Margarita Ortiz, for her life lessons of unconditional love, endurance, faith, perseverance, strength, and dedication, her culinary skills and most of all for having successfully raised four children as a single parent.

I dedicate my story to her, my role model, my rock, my everything, Margarita Ortiz. (1934 - 2018).

REFLECTION

1. Are you experiencing a hardship in your life? What are you doing to help yourself cope with it?

2. Do you have any role models who have helped shape your life?

3. What are you doing to abandon an unhealthy relationship?

BIOGRAPHY

Leonor Gil is a financial services professional with more than 30 years of experience as a Senior Vice President at a global banking institution, and as Director of Operations for Harris Associates L. P., a prominent Chicago advisory firm.

Leonor is passionate about diversity and inclusion (D&I) and has served as the Treasurer, Secretary, and Co-Chair of the Professional Development Committee of the Latino Council at Northern Trust. Leonor received Northern Trust's Chairman's Award – D&I in 2017 and the 2018 Mujeres de HACE (Women of the Hispanic Alliance for Career Enhancement) Leadership Award.

Leonor enjoys positively impacting the lives of others by volunteering for Big Brothers, Big Sister for United Way and as a Confirmation Facilitator at her church. She serves as a mentoring partner at Northern Trust and with young Latinas for The Fig Factor Foundation, where she also serves on the board.

Leonor received a B.A. degree in Finance from the University of Houston, is fluent in Spanish, holds several FINRA (Financial Industry Regulatory Authority) licenses, and has a mentor coach certification. Leonor is a proud mother of two and grandmother to four children. Her hobbies include hiking, dancing, and spending time with family.

Leonor Gil
lgil@comcast.net
(630) 202-6797

Elizabeth Villarreal

"Life's adversities give us opportunities to better ourselves."

I woke up today and realized my son is 19 years old. WOW! Is this a dream? Who am I now? Have I lost myself in the midst of motherhood? What have I become besides a mom? I am an educated, independent woman raising her son on her own. That is who I am.

My mother has always been my inspiration. She always believed in me and told me I could achieve anything I desired. She says, "Ay Liza, you are always dreaming and wanting more!" My response to her is, "*Mami*, when have you known me to not go after what I want? I will never know if I don't try!"

FAMILY ROOTS

I was born in the Pilsen neighborhood of Chicago, the youngest of nine siblings. After 16 years living in Chicago, my father wanted to move the family back to Laredo, Texas where he was originally from. My oldest siblings were all starting their own lives in Chicago and were not willing to move, so my mom remained in Chicago to raise me and the three of her youngest children on her own. I remember leaving Chicago a few years later, shortly after my fifth birthday party in October of 1976. We piled into a van with strangers, my mom, my siblings, our two dogs and headed on our journey to our new home in Laredo.

Our upbringing was humble. We had a two-bedroom home with rooms separated by curtains. Looking back now, it was a simpler life and I spoke very little Spanish. I remember meeting the neighborhood kids in the unpaved streets to play in the scorching heat. I could walk barefoot in 100-degree weather. My mother would call me *prieta*, because I was a dark child playing in my backyard with mud. I would make my own pool in the mud and jump in to cool off. My mother would have a fit, but my dad would say, "Leave her; she is happy!" I enjoyed Laredo and playing with my neighbors, who to this day are some of my dearest friends.

I was Daddy's little girl and my mother was the strict one, but she was also loving and affectionate. My siblings say I was spoiled, but I was only spoiled with love. My father wouldn't even give me a quarter to buy candy when he would send me to buy his Buglers (his favorite cigarettes). He'd say, "I don't have money." Then I would shake his pockets full of loose change and say, "Yes you do!" He would then swear like a sailor and call my mother. I do remember we both loved Kentucky Fried Chicken and a few times a year we would escape to eat a box filled with chicken, mashed potatoes, gravy, and a biscuit. That was our secret getaway and perhaps the only time I remember my father splurging on me.

On one horrible April day in 1985, my father was sweeping

up on the roof when he suffered a massive heart attack. My brother rushed up the ladder to help him, and I followed behind. He just yelled at me to get off of the roof. I can still see my father, all black and blue up to his chest.

Paramedics couldn't bring him down so they tried to resuscitate him where he was. I can still hear the banging sounds of my father trying to replace the aluminum. He died on that horrible day and my mother became a widow, left to raise her 13-year old daughter alone. She had to learn to be strong despite her pain, even as she tried to be there for her little girl who adored her father.

Growing up, I was an active teenager in the band, colorguard and choir, and I had practice every day with long hours, even on Saturdays, which is no longer allowed in Texas. My mother worked as a custodian at an elementary school and found it difficult to take me back and forth to practices, so she bought me a car in my sophomore year. I remember my beautiful, white, 1981 Ford Fairmont with red interior and the AM radio. I loved it! It was the beginning of independence.

However, none of my other siblings had ever received a car from my parents. I remember one of them whispering in my ear that I was a spoiled brat and my mother could not afford it. I never told my mom, but I could not have her supporting both the car and me. I had to find a job.

When I turned 16, I got a job at McDonald's and began to provide for myself. I was not going to take advantage of my mom like my older siblings said I did. My father always told me to never trust anyone and only depend on myself. I love my family, but I have learned never to ask for help, and I have followed my father's advice and the strong example of my mother.

It was an extremely hurtful time of my life, marred by those hateful words from my siblings, but now I realize they made me the strong woman I am today. Looking back, I realize that we never had much because we were so poor, but I always had my mother's love. I had siblings who were married and had nice cars, houses, and vacations but I was 16 and had none of that. My older siblings had my father's love for the greater part of their lives, something I will never have.

When a person speaks ill of you, remember it is motivated by jealousy from someone who is not in a happy place. I was told once to pray for those people. Praying not only heals you, it helps you forgive them.

Words are so powerful. They can bring someone down or lift them up. I was raised by a strong woman who taught me to be positive and lift myself up despite hurt and pain and that's why I think women need to know their self-worth.

UNEXPECTED BLESSINGS

After graduating high school, I continued to work, go to school, and hang out with my friends. Then one day I was asked to audition at two different radio stations by my dear friends Javier, and Sam, who were local DJs. I was hired by both stations and worked on the weekends there while I attended community college.

I was on top of the world when I was able to transfer to Texas A&M University to pursue my undergraduate degree in psychology and then my master's in physical therapy. It seemed like I had my entire life planned. Then, God blessed me with a change of plans. I was going to be a mother.

The father was a divorced man with four kids. I could clearly see he was not going to be able to support my child as well as the four he already had. That was not the life I had envisioned for myself nor my unborn child. I didn't know what to do. But when I was four months pregnant, he solved my dilemma by ending our relationship.

At first, I panicked. What was I going to do now? I was the only girl working at a tire shop with 16 wonderful coworkers. They toughened me up and made me realize I was not alone. His departure turned out to be a blessing. The last five months of pregnancy were wonderful with the support of my four best friends (Angie, Diana, Cindy, and Irene) who never left my side, and the rock of my life, my mother.

My *prieto*, my little bundle of joy, was born in January of 2000. I was working as an office manager at a national company, deejaying on the weekends and also doing voiceovers for the local TV station in Laredo. Life was good.

Then a friend told me of a job with Southwestern Bell Wireless in sales. All I heard was "sales," to which I replied, "no!" I had wanted to be a psychologist or physical therapist, never a salesperson. But I went to the interview and the manager was very convincing. Unfortunately, the salary was half of what I was currently making at only $7.50 an hour. I was afraid I could not provide for my son, but my best friend Olivia told me I would soon be making much more. I took a leap of faith, and this year I will celebrate 17 years with AT&T!

IN GOOD COMPANY

My mother always said, "Tell me who you hang out with and I will tell you who you are." I truly believe certain people are put in your path during different times in your life. We are as good as the people who surround us.

If you ask my true friends about me, they will say I am a woman who is not afraid to take chances and go after what she wants. Actually though, I am a woman who has been afraid of every single decision I have made, but I took leaps of faith and trusted God.

I am a woman who has lived a difficult journey as a single mother, but I also believe that life's adversities give us opportunities to better ourselves. Opportunities knock only once in our lives, and it is up to us to open that door and jump in with 100 percent commitment. Then we must take a leap of faith and trust in ourselves to create success. Talk to God and have faith that he will guide you in making decisions during difficult times. My advice to women is to jump at potentially life-changing experiences. It's better to fail than never try at all and always wonder what would have happened.

I have taken chances throughout my life to gain opportunity for me and my son. We moved to San Antonio, Texas in 2008 when he was eight years old and in the third grade. We didn't know a soul there, but we made great friends and I was able to finish my education, receiving a bachelor's degree in marketing from the University of Phoenix.

In 2015, we moved to Chicago to be closer to family and for my career. Unfortunately, I was laid off in 2016 and had 60 days to find a job. Friends from AT&T always told me there was life after leaving, but I had 15 years invested and had wanted to retire from there! Still, I had faith God would provide for us. On day 60, a woman interviewed me, and I was hired to do a job I first did 15 years ago. In retrospect, losing my job led me to become a stronger woman who is grateful for everything she has. I'm learning to focus more on what I have rather than what I don't.

Remember, adversities will come your way, people will speak ill of you, but it will only destroy you if you let it. I always try to keep my head up high and keep smiling. Show them the amazing journey you are on and watch out, because God continues to provide amazing opportunities. I have been honored to have the opportunity to be part of this book and I am now surrounded by amazing, positive, and inspiring Latina women. Stay tuned!

REFLECTION

1. Has anyone ever used words against you? How did you react?

2. Have you ever taken a leap of faith? Who did you trust to help you?

3. Do you see adversity as a positive or negative thing?

BIOGRAPHY

Elizabeth Villarreal is a Client Sales Executive with AT&T. She received her BS in Marketing at the University of Phoenix, and is currently working on her MBA.

She serves on several boards and is the VP of Operations for HACEMOS, an employee resource group of AT&T that aligns with her passion of giving back to the Latino community. HACEMOS raises money for scholarships, promotes higher education, and sets up STEM programs for high school students in the Chicago area.

Elizabeth also recently joined the board of the Fig Factor Foundation, an organization that unleashes the amazing in young Latinas. She serves as chair for the Music Parent Association board at Hinsdale Central High School, where she enjoys volunteering and watching her son sing in the choir.

She is the mother of two sons: Robert, who is 19 and a senior in high school, and her six-year-old, four- legged little boy named Jake.

Elizabeth Villareal
lizalove.latina@gmail.com
(210) 332-6809

Denisse Robledo

"As long as we are breathing, we're a work in progress, and we should embrace the journey."

From a young age, I knew I could overcome any obstacle in front of me. I was a smart, creative, and ambitious kid. At times I was a little unfocused, but definitely a go-getter. I knew that no matter what life threw my way, I would always land on my feet. I can't count the number of times my mother told me, "I don't worry about you, Denisse. You're a survivor and you'll always figure it out."

My family moved to the United States when I was six years old. We didn't speak a word of English, but my brother and I became fluent in a matter of months, soaking up the language like it was made for us. I was raised by a single mother, and my family didn't have very much money, yet despite my circumstances, I did well in school and participated in a lot of extracurricular activities like theater, dance, and sports.

My mother, attempting to navigate a new culture and language, didn't have the resources to support our endeavors but always found a way to make it happen. She encouraged our exposure to anything that would develop us into more fully-realized individuals.

Growing up in Kansas City, Missouri, I never felt like I belonged, and I wanted to be in a larger city with more noise, culture, and exciting opportunities. It didn't matter that we had no way to pay for it; I was determined to go away for college.

SHE PERSISTED

I fought hard to earn a scholarship to DePaul University and was elated when they offered to pay the majority of my tuition. Moving to Chicago was a dream come true. The city felt alive with an energy I found intoxicating and I acclimated to the pace of life there almost instantly. I was young, filled with hope and possibility, and excited to dream about what I wanted my new life to look like.

I graduated from college in 2003 and held a few professional jobs, learning how to navigate the complex social environment of corporate America all on my own. None of these positions had anything to do with my degree, but that didn't dissuade me. I felt like I was on the right path and would eventually find my way.

Everything I had worked for was on track...sort of. I had a good job that I didn't exactly love (or was passionate about, if I'm being honest) but I was gainfully employed, my boyfriend and I were in love, I was living on my own and "adulting successfully." Then one day in 2008, right as our country was entering a recession, it was all pulled out from under me. I got called into my manager's office and told I was being let go. It came as a shock (but also as somewhat of a relief). I told myself it was going to be alright and that I would land on my feet like I always had.

The next few months I applied to more than 100 job postings, often getting called in for second and third interviews, but never receiving an offer. My situation continued to grow more serious and one day I checked my bank account and learned I had $15 to my name. Those were very difficult months and there were days I wasn't sure how I was going to eat or scrounge up enough to pay my rent. I was able to piece together a couple of part-time jobs to keep myself afloat, but I couldn't help feeling like my progress had come to an abrupt halt.

A few months later, I discovered I was pregnant and was overcome with anxiety that I was about to bring a child into a life that was less than ideal. I was uninsured and had to quickly learn how to navigate the Illinois Public Aid system, something I was ashamed to admit for a long time because of the stigma attached to it. I couldn't reconcile how I was a 28-year-old college graduate with nothing to show for myself. At that moment, the life I had pictured when I moved to Chicago seemed unattainable.

My mother and grandmother both came to the United States and suffered great hardships to give their family a better life. My mother had a successful career in Mexico, but none of that mattered when she arrived in the United States. She suffered discrimination, endured poor working conditions, and never earned more than minimum wage. Because her sense of duty to her family was so strong, she never complained and always found a way to make sure my brother and I had everything we needed. The only thing she ever demanded of me was that I try my best.

I've always felt a great sense of responsibility to my mother and grandmother for their unrelenting sacrifices. Finding myself so far from my dreams felt like I was dishonoring their legacy and everything they had worked so hard to give me. This wasn't how my life was supposed to go and I felt like a failure.

GIRL INTERRUPTED

My daughter was born on a sunny Thursday in September of 2009. The feeling I got when we met for the first time was indescribable, but in that moment, I understood the love my mother and grandmother had for me and I knew that I would follow in their footsteps. When my daughter was 18 months old, her father and I married in a beautiful ceremony surrounded by friends and loved ones. My husband continues to be my best friend and biggest supporter to this day.

I worked as a stay-at-home mom until my daughter was two and a half and that was the most difficult job I've ever held. I loved the time I spent with my beautiful little girl and will forever treasure those memories, but it was also very isolating, and I suffered from terrible anxiety and postpartum depression. I remember waiting for the "baby blues" to pass, but relief never came. Weeks turned into months, and I found myself overcome with hopelessness, having daily crying spells and unable to get out of bed or complete simple tasks. I felt like I was drowning and failing as a wife and a mother.

Growing up, mental illness was not something that was openly discussed or even acknowledged in my household. I was socialized to be eternally self-sacrificing, always putting the needs of others before my own, even if it meant having nothing left to give to myself. As a result, I felt guilt and shame about what I was going through, which only served to exacerbate my condition. I didn't yet understand that it's possible to love your child, love motherhood and feel depressed at the same time.

At times it was like I was watching myself from the outside, looking in. I wanted to reach out and pull myself out of my despair, shake myself and say, "snap out of it!" but I didn't know how. Finally, one day my husband sat me down and helped me realize that I needed to seek professional treatment.

The thought of making an appointment was daunting, but I eventually did it. There were days I had to force myself out of the house, but I began attending weekly sessions with a therapist. With some nudging from a friend, I also joined a running group. All of it was exhausting, but I told myself to just put one foot in front of the other and focus on the next step (literally and figuratively). Little by little, I started to feel like I was coming out of my dark place. It took months to build trust with my therapist, but once I opened up, she helped me understand some of the emotional stress and past trauma I'd been carrying around for years and how it was manifesting itself as depression. Most importantly, she taught me how to let go and forgive myself for all my perceived failures, unmet expectations, and the pressure I was putting on myself.

BECOMING

Recovery is an ongoing process. Since coming out of the

worst of my depression, I've returned to the workforce and have built a successful career in a creative field that I love. It hasn't always been easy. I had to learn how to navigate a professional environment again but now in a faster, more agile, and tech-savvy world. Sometimes those old thought patterns have crept back in and I've found myself battling Imposter Syndrome, or the feeling that I'm really a fraud. I've had to work really hard at developing a growth mindset and understanding that I am a continual work in progress.

One of the best and most rewarding experiences I've had was working for a locally headquartered company that allowed me to grow both personally and professionally. I'd been eyeing their job postings for over 12 months before a friend helped me get my foot in the door for an interview.

I started out at the very bottom but was just so happy to be there that I continued to show up every day with a good attitude, a strong work ethic, and an unshakable determination to make a name for myself. It paid off, and I received several promotions within a relatively short period of time, all while maintaining a good work-life balance. I was proud of the strides I was making in my career, but more importantly, I was proud of the example that I was setting for my daughter. Not just as a woman working outside of the home and providing for her family, but also as a woman who prioritizes her well-being and makes time for self-care.

I love the life that my family and I have created. It didn't always follow the path that I had envisioned or dreamed about in my younger years. The twists, turns, and detours were challenging, and I almost lost myself trying to force things to stay "on course." Today I feel proud of my journey because it's made me the woman I am —someone who makes their mother, grandmother, and daughter very proud.

PERFECTLY IMPERFECT

In the age of perfectly curated Instagram grids, I want women to understand that it's ok to be a hot mess sometimes and not always have it "all together." It's ok if your house is not Pinterest-perfect or you don't wear a size 0. It's ok to make some stumbles in your career along the way. Most importantly, it's ok to not be ok and have to ask for help. You don't have to suffer in silence or alone.

We have a tendency to place arbitrary deadlines and expectations on ourselves for how we want our lives to look but when life inevitably doesn't go according to plan, we end up suffering disappointment or despair. I've had to learn to let go of those timelines and remind myself that as long as we are breathing, we're a work in progress and we should embrace the journey. Sometimes we're closer to our goals and the life that we want and other times we still have work to do.

The most important thing I've learned so far is to never stop learning and to ask for help when it's needed. Being a survivor doesn't mean having to navigate those rough waters on your own. As long as we adapt the attitude that there's still time to learn something we haven't learned yet, there will exist the possibility to achieve something we haven't achieved *yet*.

REFLECTION

1. What do you need help with right now?

2. What is one step you can take to minimize the stigma of mental illness in your community?

3. Are you holding yourself to any arbitrary deadlines? How can you let go and allow life and achievements to come in their own time?

BIOGRAPHY

Denisse Robledo is a Creative Producer specializing in still and motion digital media. That's a fancy way of saying she loves telling stories through pictures and video. She is currently part of the production team at Crate & Barrel and loves helping bring such an iconic brand to life.

Denisse was born in Monterrey, Mexico, raised in Kansas City, and currently resides in Chicago with her husband and daughter. A feminist since the womb, her passion for empowering women has led Denisse to sit on various boards and committees, most recently for the Chicago chapter of The Latinista® network. She is working on launching a podcast, "Cocktails con Comadres" to foster a supportive community and provide Latinas a platform to share their experiences.

In 2017, Denisse was accepted to compete in the Hackathon at the Massachusetts Institute of Technology's Media Lab, taking home first place with her team for the Artists Challenge. Not one to sit still for very long, Denisse has played and coached roller derby for the Windy City Rollers, is a former marathon runner, and has even trained for a bodybuilding competition. She is currently seeking her next great adventure.

Denisse Robledo
denissechapa@gmail.com
773-717-9352

I AM...

Claudia Vazquez

"Surround yourself with those who believe in the beauty of your dreams."

I welcome you to read this vignette as I fill in the blanks of the various stages of my life and invite you to think through your own journey and reignite, or discover for the first time, the passion within you. It's the one thing that makes you joyful that you could do all day long. That is IT! Pursue it and then you will finally be who YOU are meant to be!

My beginning may be slightly different from other Latinas living in the U.S. today. My parents are originally from Mexico. They met and got married in Pasadena, California, where I was born. However, because of their patriotism and desire for their only daughter to know her roots, we moved to Guadalajara Jalisco, Mexico. My parents got divorced when I was three, but my father was always present in my life. I lived with my mother, my beloved grandmother and my cousin. I attended an all-girls, very strict, Catholic, bilingual school. In January of 1980, at the young age of nine, my life took its first shocking turn.

Every year, during the Christmas break, we would go to Pasadena to visit my aunts from mid-December to the first week of January. We would visit famous amusement parks, go to cabins in the snowy mountains, buy our year's supply of clothes and even get the newest doll, which tended to be the envy of my classmates. I was a regular, middle-class girl but with advantages that others did not have. Well, that January was different.

My mother got a very bad cold, and she told me we would stay a few extra days in California while she recovered. I was so excited to spend more time with her and my aunts. Little did I know!

When my aunts took my grandmother (their mom) to the airport, my mother broke the news to me. We were not going back to Guadalajara. She had decided to move to Ensenada, Baja California, in the northern part of Mexico, and she had already sold all our furniture. All we had was what we carried in our two pieces of luggage.

My heart broke and I remember screaming and crying and feeling completely devastated. I could not breathe at the thought of being so far away from my father, grandma, cousins, friends, and everything I knew! How was I going to live in a city I hadn't visited before? How was I going to overcome this pain? I cried myself to sleep that night.

I AM DIFFERENT

Joining a new school and living in a new community, in a new city, is not easy! Even though I was in the same country, my accent was different. The words I used were from the south of Mexico, not the north. I went from an all-girls Catholic school to a mixed school at a time when bullying was a common practice. Boys would make fun of girls and even more so if their accent was different. But I survived, became resilient and self-sufficient, and I matured. In no time, I had created my new ecosystem of friends and was enjoying my new life. Little did I know that when I turned 13, I would have to do it all again.

This time, my mother thought it would be good for me to move to Pasadena with my aunt to practice my English and learn about American history. After all, I was American, wasn't I? Well, in January of 1984, I moved to Pasadena with my aunt, and once again I experienced the pain of separation and the feeling of abandonment. Once again, I activated my qualities of resilience, maturity, and self-sufficiency to help me in the transition.

I was now placed in ESL (English as a second language) classes with kids from all over the world. My classes had students from Vietnam, the Philippines, Armenia, Mexico, El Salvador, Guatemala, Colombia, etc. with a mixture of cultures, races, and some languages that were all new to me.

Once again, I was different from the majority and I refused to take all ESL classes. I figured if my purpose in going to California was to practice English, then I needed to attend my classes in English! So without informing my aunt (who was my guardian), I took a risk and asked the principal and the educational director for permission to be transferred to regular English classes, even though I knew it would be a struggle. Nowadays, with Google translate, doing homework in English would be a breeze! But then, I knew it would take me a lot longer to finish my homework because I would have to use the English/ Spanish dictionary.

That school year, as well as the following one, I managed to complete some honors classes, where I earned mostly A's and B's. My group of friends grew exponentially, as I had the ability to navigate between the ESL students and the all-English speakers.

Because I had branched out into the all-English classes, I was regarded as a leader within our multicultural peer group. This 18-month experience helped me become disciplined and focused. I took more risks, developed my leadership skills, and quickly assimilated to my new environment.

Between the age of 15 and now, I have lived in six cities within Mexico, the U.S., and Canada. Every time we moved, my ability to adapt and embrace new experiences improved. Consequently, I feel like a master at change management!

I AM A SERVANT LEADER

In January of 1994, I became engaged to the love of my life. In March of 1994, we got married. Talk about taking a risk! We only dated 11 months, and I left my job, my family, my friends, and my education to marry him and move to a paradise, which I will describe shortly.

My husband is a physician and as part of his bachelor's degree program, all Mexican physicians are required to complete one year of social service in a rural area before they can graduate. Therefore, we moved to Zipolite, Oaxaca, a nudist beach in the southern part of Mexico. Yes, you read it right. Nudist! Since we were considered locals, we could use regular clothing which was a huge relief!

In our new location, there were no phones or running water in the village and most houses had dirt floors. We were very lucky because we lived in the small clinic. We had a small private room and bathroom with the most beautiful view of the ocean. We lived just steps from the beach.

The first two weeks were a true honeymoon. I took naps, walked by the beach and read, while my husband worked in consultations from 9 to 5. But after two weeks, I started to get anxious with so much free time. So, I started to think about what I could do. I had only worked at McDonald's as a cashier and at State Farm as a sales representative, which provided no transferable skills for Zipolite, but I spoke English and the town received many tourists from the U.S. and Europe.

I decided to become an ESL teacher for elementary school children. I created my own materials by cutting images from magazines and pasting them onto cardboard. I marketed my classes at the clinic and I soon had 10 elementary children enrolled for class every Monday and Wednesday, with middle school students on Tuesdays and Thursdays.

During the day, I helped my husband in the clinic. I learned to give vaccinations, delivered babies at his side, and completed medical history reports that were due at the end of the month. It was then that I realized my calling was to help others succeed. This 12-month experience helped me become creative, tenacious, and more compassionate.

FROM I AM NOT ENOUGH TO I AM TOTALLY WORTH IT!

In January of 1996, we decided to permanently move to Pasadena, California for several reasons. First, I could finish my bachelor's degree, which I had always dreamed of doing, but hadn't due to finances and the relocations.

Upon arriving in Pasadena, I visited the closest community college campus and took several placement tests. My English score was very low so the counselor recommended multiple English classes.

To make a long story short, I ultimately realized that unless I had a clear goal and a plan to achieve it, I would not succeed. So, I created a master plan and began to diligently work towards it. It took me six years to finish my bachelor's degree while working full time, being pregnant with our first child and managing the purchase of our first home. I also followed my calling to help others succeed by volunteering as an ESL teacher and a citizenship instructor. More than 80 Hispanic students achieved their U.S. citizenship by attending my classes at a local community center, making my efforts totally worth it! When I graduated from the community college, all my students came and I had the loudest cheers when I walked across the stage to receive my diploma. They were just as happy and proud as my own family because I was fulfilling the dreams they had for their own children.

The feelings of not being "enough" and not even "college material" came to mind several times throughout those six years, whenever I couldn't understand certain economic concepts, statistical regression analysis, or computer coding. Or when I applied to an amazing Fortune 500 company and was hired at a 20 percent lower salary because I had not finished my degree. I did not quit or blame anyone. I did not stop pursuing my ultimate dream. On the contrary, I persevered, pushed through, got up every morning, remained positive, and was determined and diligent. It is all about grit and attitude!

At the age of 30, I arrived at my desired destination when we had our first son. Forty days later, I graduated with a degree in psychology. The trans-generational cycle was broken; I became the first one in my family to graduate from college!

I went on to complete a master's degree, and by the time I was 35, I was managing 22 people, pregnant with my second child, and starting to live the life I had imagined. Since then, I have received multiple promotions and growth opportunities, as well as national recognition for the impact I have had in the community and for being a diversity and inclusion leader wherever I go. In January of 2016, I founded Univerbond Camp, designed to inspire children and adults in the pursuit of their dreams by following the five keys to success.

I found my passion and have achieved many dreams! But I could not have done it without the support of my husband, my family, friends, encouraging managers, mentors, and co-workers. It takes a village. Surround yourself with those who believe in the beauty of your dreams!

WHO AM I? I AM ME!

This January was different. First, I am not physically moving to a new place, but I'm moving forward spiritually. I am mindful of myself. I am writing a summary of my personal story with the feeling of certainty that everything in my past has made me the best version of myself. This version is stronger, more creative, willing to take risks and dream, and willing to bring other women along to experience success and joy and inspire them to mentor other Hispanics too.

I am the wife of Dr. Francisco Vazquez and the mom of Axel, Enzo, and Ian. I am Alicia and Salvador's daughter, Andrea's sister and a friend to Dina, Karla, Virginia, Alice, Juliet, and Sylvia. I am a mentor and a godmother. I am all those things, but I am no longer defined by a title, my role in society, or a relationship. I am unique in every sense of the word. I am genuinely happy and enough, just being me. I am Claudia, and my true journey is just getting started.

REFLECTION

1. How would you describe your passion?
2. Who are the people who have encouraged you to keep going? Do you have a strong ecosystem of people who believe in your dreams?
3. What painful experiences have made you the best version of yourself?

BIOGRAPHY

Claudia Vazquez, MAOM, LSSBB, is a Director, Product Management, of Prudential's Group Insurance. Claudia is focused on expanding products and improving disability market position. From 2015-18, Claudia supervised Prudential's Africa, Europe, and Latin American region compliance teams.

Claudia has 20 years of insurance experience. Prior to joining Prudential, she had a proven, progressive career in group insurance leadership positions and managed operational claim teams of more than 100 people working in various U.S. regions for State Farm, Unum, and Cigna.

Claudia earned a B.A. in Psychology and an M.A. in Organizational Management. She holds certifications in project management, Six Sigma Black Belt and as an Agile professional since 2018.

Currently, Claudia is the Hispanic Initiatives Officer of JUNTOS (Prudential's Hispanic Business Resource Group) and sits on the advisory board for Prospanica New Jersey and Latino Network Coalition. In 2018, Claudia received the Hispanics Inspiring Student Performance and Achievement's (HISPA) Champion of the Year award and in 2007 she was awarded Hispanic Association on Corporate Responsibility's (HACR) Young Hispanic Corporate Achiever award in Washington DC.

Claudia founded Univerbond Camp, and facilitates workshops designed to connect imagination, action, and gratitude to deliver successful results.

Claudia Vazquez
claudiavazquez.inspiredlatina@gmail.com
www.univerbondcamp.com
(626) 577-1540

UNORTHODOX LATINA

Monica Lopez

"Be the role model you wish you had."

I grew up with mixed roots, a blend of city and the 'burbs. In my younger years, I lived in "Little Village" in Chicago and then in the south suburbs from childhood through adulthood. Though different, they both had challenges.

I dropped out of high school in the first semester of my junior year because I experienced a lack of support in the school system, including inequity in the classroom and socioeconomic and racial discrimination. At a young age, it was very evident to me that no matter how long I lived in the suburbs, how much my parents paid in property taxes, or even how "American" I was, it just didn't matter. What mattered most was that I was Latina, and being a Latina somehow put me at a disadvantage.

I signed up for GED classes almost immediately, and my life became retail work and night school. I began to feel empty. I would ask myself, *is this what my life is supposed to be?* Then one night, while sitting in my GED class, I looked around and noticed the room was filled with minorities and a few white people. It was then I realized I had given up my right to equality. I returned to high school the following semester.

GIRL ON FIRE

Upon my return I was told, "Monica, you won't be able to graduate on stage with your class. You will have to take classes at a community college two nights a week. You will have to start your days at seven o'clock in the morning, take a "zero hour" class before the start of the standard school day. Oh, and you will have to go to summer school." WOW!!

That would have scared many people away, but I had returned to school in full force. I was stronger than ever and determined to rise. The value of education had been instilled in me very early on thanks to my mother. It was her belief that learning should never stop. As a result, I spent many summers studying for hours at time. Learning was in my DNA, but up until high school graduation, I didn't have the self-awareness of my true strength or the belief that I knew enough to achieve anything I wanted.

When I was presented with my high school diploma, it was a surreal moment I shared with my mom. We knew I had accomplished so much more than just the diploma and so did the school principal and counselor who presented it to me. If I had a dollar for every surprised expression on their faces, I'd be a millionaire! They didn't think I would complete the extra work to graduate, but the opportunity to prove them wrong had driven me to succeed.

I started college immediately after graduation, but what I didn't know was that I was already a college student! I already had college credits on my transcript that counted towards my first semester from the evening classes I had taken at the local community college.

I don't remember anyone sharing that piece of information when they were listing the things I needed for high school graduation. Maybe they didn't expect me to go to college?

I had an interesting start to my community college journey. You may question my choice of words (i.e. journey), but it took me 10 years to complete community college. I think that qualifies as a journey!

In college, there were no support groups or systems in place to help minority students be successful, just as there were none in high school. Imagine trying to navigate the process alone, then have to hear, "Oh by the way, you have to take placement tests to see what courses you are able to take."

The tests basically determined whether you were going to be a traditional two-year or what I like to call a "long-term" community college student. So I took the test and when the results were in, I had placed well in all subjects except math.

I stayed positive, but despite my good attitude, I desperately struggled. I dropped the remedial math course six times and failed it twice. Today, students continue to struggle and higher education system models have not changed enough to help all students succeed. I continued to wrestle with remedial courses, self-esteem, time management, and balancing my school, home, and work life.

I was no stranger to hard work so I willingly put in the dedication needed after dropping the math class for one last time. I lived in the tutoring center, used up my teacher's office hours, and was the first to class and the last one to leave. I had many moments where I doubted myself and questioned whether I could go on to a university. In the end, I completed community college and realized my biggest fear was behind me. I entered my undergraduate program on fire! This time around, I finished in two years.

Getting my undergraduate degree was very special to me because of the sacrifices I made and the many evenings spent away from my family. I practically lived on campus and spent many months driving there twice a day because of my family responsibilities. Many nights, I stayed up until four o'clock in the morning writing papers and doing homework on the weekend.

Remember, I was not a standard student; I had a family of my own. I had no time to make new friends or join clubs or organizations. Role models who I could identify with were scarce or non-existent. The career center was useless and offered zero opportunities for students who were more experienced in the workforce. I was completely on my own, eager to embark on my new career, with little guidance.

In the end, I took what I could from my experience and before I knew it, it was the last day of classes. I took my last final exam and sped to my mom's house to pick up my son. Then I went home and cried, cradling him in my arms.

I knew that deep down I did it for him, so he would never feel alone and he wouldn't have to search for a role model. I am the first person in my family to graduate with a four-year degree, and I'm also the eldest daughter of my parents and the first grandchild to my grandparents. Throughout my journey, I always remembered the sacrifices my family had made to elevate their children so they could have a better future. I was determined to create a path for my children that would eliminate the obstacles that I faced as a student and young professional.

Graduation day arrived. As I walked across that stage, my undergraduate journey flashed before my eyes, and in that flash, was my family. It was then that I understood the value and magnitude of my accomplishment. I could never have made it without their support.

FOLLOW "YOUR" YELLOW BRICK ROAD

Society gives us a blueprint for following a traditional path. Family gives us values that may or may not align with that blueprint. The path usually includes high school graduation, followed by a college degree, decent-paying employment, finding a spouse, having children, and buying a house. Unfortunately, the blueprint is not a universal fit. I dropped out of high school, chose to get pregnant at 19, became a long-term community college student, got married after I had my son, bought the property, and then attained my four-year college degree.

One day, I sat with my dad reflecting on life. He said to me, "Gosh, Monica, you really did it all backwards." I looked at him and said, "Dad, life doesn't hand you a straight path; it's full of winding roads. I did not stay on the yellow brick road, but you are the only one in your family who can say you have a daughter with a bachelor's degree. I'd say I turned out even better!"

Today, I am a college graduate with a successful career, and an author, speaker, entrepreneur, advocate for women, community contributor, influencer, mentor, and cancer survivor. The truth is that a perfect path does not exist. In the *Wizard of Oz*, Dorothy followed the yellow brick road but it couldn't prepare her for everything ahead. It only pointed her in a general direction. Also, she still hit a point in her journey where the road split into two directions.

On Memorial Day in 2016, I lost my best friend of 17 years to a fatal car accident. Six months later, precisely two days before Christmas, I was diagnosed with metastatic thyroid cancer at the age of 33. I was at the height of my career, and life had thrown a wrecking ball at me. Emotionally, I was broken and grieving the loss of my best friend. I felt empty, angry, and confused. Physically, I was very fatigued and in pain. Psychologically, I was barely functioning. It was a time in my life when I realized nobody could help me. I had to enter a soul-searching journey alone.

I realized that in life you can follow a yellow brick road, but life can split your path and completely derail you. I had two choices: (1) sit there and feel sorry for myself, go into a deep depression and wake when it was over, or (2) turn the situation into the opportunity to become the inspiring role model I never had.

BE ONE WITH YOUR WHY

Growing up, I didn't know what a role model was, or how

to identify one. When I entered the workforce, I could not find Latino organizations that could help me develop professionally or help me have some kind of impact. In 2016, I was introduced to the Association of Latino Professionals for America (ALPHA), a 45-year-old-year old, national organization that was very prominent in Chicago. I wondered where this organization was when I was just starting out! I said to myself, *Ok, Monica, this is an opportunity to be the role model you wish you had.*

My "why" was to help Latinos in my community connect with organizations that had resources to help them advance professionally. ALPHA shaped my leadership, volunteerism, and brought me back full circle to my "why." I got involved in multiple areas of the organization and helped out wherever I could, no matter how menial the task. Today, as a board member on our Chicago board and a national ambassador, I have been able to expand our impact by opening the doors for Latinos across the country to connect and engage with leaders, role models, and mentors like myself. I am committed to creating visibility and accessibility to resources and professional development that will help advance Latinos and build career pathways for students and professionals on a grand scale. I am a servant leader of the community, delivering unique educational and professional development opportunities to students and professionals. I am an advocate for woman and championing equity in education, entrepreneurship, and the workforce.

Always remember, it is never too late to identify organizations that you can impact, and no contribution is too small. Your "why" is just as important as your work ethic and talent. Your "why" should be the center of everything that you do; it is your compass to success. You never know what part of your journey will spark the fire to something greater. The great Ruby Dee once said, "The world has improved mostly because unorthodox people did unorthodox things. Not surprisingly, they had the courage and daring to think they could make a difference."

REFLECTION

1. Are you self-aware of what sets your soul on fire?

2. Have you found opportunity in unorthodox experiences?

3. What is your "why" and have you become one with your "why?"

BIOGRAPHY

Monica Lopez is a human resources-organizational development professional, and an author, speaker, entrepreneur, advocate for women, community contributor, influencer, mentor, and cancer survivor. Monica is passionate about empowering women to embrace their authenticity, build on their talent and design a professional experience that elevates them personally and professionally.

Monica has turned her adversities into opportunities to expand her reach among women. She advocates for women fighting for equity in education and the workplace. Her work and speaking experience have empowered women to take charge of their personal and professional development and advocate for themselves in the workplace.

Monica has a B.A. in Human Resource and Organizational Development and 10 years of experience in human resources and professional development. Her experience in higher education inspires many first-generation Latinos to navigate their educational journey with Latino leadership support. Monica champions diversity and inclusion in higher education and has worked with non-profit and private organizations to deliver programming that advances Latino professionals and brings Latino talent to organizations.

She is a board member for ALPHA Chicago and an ambassador for ALPHA National, and a council member for the Advocacy, Quality Jobs and Adult College Success Council for Women Employed.

Monica Lopez
latinaandco@gmail.com
(708) 745-4510

TRANSFORM YOUR DISADVANTAGES INTO
OPPORTUNITIES FOR SUCCESS

Ruby Botello

"Appreciate what you have, work hard, and never give up."

I grew up in the city of Chicago in a low to middle-class family and was the middle child of two immigrant parents. Like many other immigrants, my parents were able to escape from a life of poverty and little opportunity and enter a life of poverty with *greater* opportunity. My family struggled to make ends meet, but by the grace of God and the generosity of other family members and friends, we always had food on the table and a coat to wear during the cold winter days.

However "poor" we were, there was never a lack of love and support in my family, which made us rich in my heart. Growing up underprivileged has been a blessing for me because it taught me how to appreciate what I have, to work hard, and to never give up. I believe that these qualities have been foundational to my success as an entrepreneur. As you read my story, my hope is that it will inspire and empower you to charge toward your goals and aspirations when you have an unwavering desire to succeed, knowing you are supported along the way when you put your heart behind your work.

Throughout my story, there will be *Moments of Reflection* where I will ask you to reflect on life events that you may have interpreted as set backs, losses, or disadvantages. Has there been a point in your life where you felt victimized? Let's look for the silver lining. I've had "tragedies" and disadvantages in life, but in my story, I will show you how I have transformed them into advantages and opportunities for self-growth and success.

GOOD FROM BAD

In the summer of 2002, my father was involved in a work-related accident where he severely damaged both his feet and had to have immediate reconstructive surgery. My father was the breadwinner of the house, and my mother stayed at home to care for my mentally handicapped, younger sister. I was 15 years old and immediately took out a work permit in order to be able to contribute to my family's well-being. The doctors said it would take at least six months for my father to be able to stand on his own two feet (literally). This tragic event in my family's life compelled me to enter the workforce and help support my family.

The company that my father worked for did look out for my family's best interest, and they were able to help my father get money through a workman's compensation policy. The money he received definitely did not compensate for having to deal with living the rest of his life with screws in his feet. Nevertheless, it was enough money to help me start my own business in 2011, nine years later.

My father invested his money in me. I was 23, bold, young,

and fearless, with the strength and hard work ethic of my father and the same heart and hands of gold that my mother had. Looking back, if my father had not been injured, he would not have received any money. I would not have had the opportunity to start my business at such a young age, yet in doing so he gave me a successful start very early in life. *Moment of Reflection:* Can you recall an unexpected event in your life that ended up being beneficial for you? What was it and how were you positively impacted?

Life does not make any mistakes. I believe there is an order to life and that we are always on the right path. If you are currently not where you want to be, be patient with your journey. Perhaps there are things you still need to learn, people you still need to meet, and mistakes you still need to make in order to make you wiser.

Before I started my business, I worked at different spas and wellness centers. It was there I learned how to run a successful business by following amazing examples of leadership, ethical business practices, and five-star customer service structures. It was also there where I observed and found examples of bad leadership, and examples of how NOT to run a business. It is important to remain humble and learn from both the good and bad experiences in life, because at the end of the day, these experiences become your greatest teachers.

I did not earn a master's degree in business. I also did not go to college. I am not advocating for you not to go to school or saying that it is not important to go to college. I do want to say that being a successful entrepreneur is not solely based on having a degree. I have still received an education.

I attended various business seminars from trusted leading authorities like John Demartini, Tony Robbins, Vishen Lakhiani and Deepak Chopra and I read all the books I can get my hands on to brainwash myself to be successful. I joke about that, but many of us are not born with the positive thinking, high-achieving mentality needed to help you become a successful entrepreneur. It takes time, energy, effort, desire, and heart to get yourself there if you really, really want it! I know you can, if I can! *Moment of Reflection:* What negative work-related experiences have you encountered and how have they positively impacted you in your career today?

FINDING THE "WHY"

One of the most important things you must have in order to accomplish what you set out to do is a deep, driving, desire to succeed. Think of what your "why" is. Your *"why"* should include something bigger than just wanting to make a lot of money. Your desire should be in alignment with your heart and belief system. Becoming a successful entrepreneur also requires a strong work ethic, a significant investment of your time, and an uncompromising drive to reach your dream.

For me, having a strong work ethic meant waking up early every single day and staying late in order to build a consistent routine and solid framework that fostered success. I showed up to my wellness studio every day at least an hour before my scheduled "open" time, even if I had no booked appointments on that day. It can be heartbreaking to show up to work and not have anything on your schedule for that whole day, and then have to go back again the next day. BUT it is crucial to show up, nonetheless! Don't give up! Successful entrepreneurs are successful because they never quit. There were days when I wanted to throw in the towel, but remembering why I started kept me motivated and fueled me to continue and move forward toward success.

When I go to Mexico to visit my family, I look around at all the poverty and feel so grateful and blessed that my parents made the decision to move to a new country despite the foreign language and little to no emotional support there. They came anyway, with only twenty dollars in their pocket.

When I reflect on that, I realize that my parents already did most of the hard work for my family. I humbly take on a leadership role to continue to move them forward. Family is everything to me and has been my biggest reason to succeed. It is important for you to have a deep, driving desire to succeed. I desire to leave a legacy for my family now, here in the U.S.; for my family back home in Mexico; and for my future family for generations to come. *Moment of Reflection:* Take a moment to reflect on your "why."

LIFE IS NOT GUARANTEED

I believe we are born into this life to learn from our mistakes, grow from our failures, and evolve to become the best version of ourselves possible. Life is so very precious and delicate.

We are not guaranteed tomorrow. All we have is the possibility of today. I have always felt this in my heart, but it wasn't until June 13, 2016, the day my entire existence suddenly collapsed, and my spiritual beliefs were put to the test.

My beloved husband of four years, the father of my two precious baby boys, unexpectedly went into cardiac arrest. Soon after being rushed to the emergency room, he was pronounced dead. He was only 31 years old.

I share this with urgency to help you realize that your life can change in a day. You are alive! Make the best of the life you are privileged to live. Don't wait for tomorrow to follow your dreams. Book that vacation, run that marathon, quit that job you are so unhappy with, and follow your passion. Don't take your family and friends for granted. Take care of them and tell them you love them. This experience connected me even deeper with my spirituality. My heart burst open and my eyes opened wide. I was showered with unconditional love from my family, friends, and even strangers.

Reflecting back, I could have easily given up on my business and allowed this tragic experience to take the best of me. Instead, I chose to channel the grief and pain into passion and purpose for my life and I tripled my business over the next two years! This experience connected me even deeper with my spirituality and the understanding that our time and our health are our most valuable resources. *Moment of Reflection:* What are some things you would love to accomplish but have not because you feel you don't have time? If you were given 30 days to live, what would you prioritize? Now, create that list and make it happen!

If you only remember one thing from everything I have shared with you, please remember this - it all starts with setting an intention! If you want to create and manifest the life of your dreams, you must have the intention to do it. Our intentions set the blueprint for the things we desire to come to fruition. If I had never set the intention to open up my own business, I would not have done it.

Of course, we need to take action in order to set everything in motion. There are no limits except those we impose on ourselves. I have realized that the more love I have for myself, the more worthy I feel about receiving God's blessings in my life. We are all worthy of living the life we desire. The only thing that can stop us is ourselves.

I have shared my story of success with you, including the most challenging times in my life. I could have used them as an excuse to fail, but instead I have used them as an opportunity to excel. My life is not over yet and there are many other accomplishments I plan to achieve. I want to open up more wellness studios in the future and plan on marrying and forming a family once again.

There is no better time than now to be an inspired Latina! We are unstoppable! When we set our hearts and minds to do something, there is nothing we can't accomplish! There is power in unity and love. Whatever your limiting beliefs are, whatever challenges you think are blocking you from obtaining your dreams, I ask you to change the way you look at them. Transform them into opportunities that will help you make your dreams come true!!

REFLECTION

1. What can you do to appreciate life, right here, right now?

2. Do you know your "why?"

3. Have you ever set an intention to achieve something you've always wanted to accomplish? What happened?

BIOGRAPHY

Ruby Botello is a Mexican Latina entrepreneur, born and raised in the city of Chicago. She is a Clinical Massage Therapist, Reiki Master and owner of Massage Evolved, a massage and beauty wellness studio located in the downtown West Loop neighborhood of Chicago.

Ruby is fascinated by philosophy, spirituality, and quantum physics. Although raised Catholic, she believes we all come from the same source and are connected through the same powerful and invisible force. Her life mission is to study and understand the human mind, body, and spirit. By understanding these three aspects of ourselves, she believes we can better comprehend the nature of reality, shape our present, and create our future.

When Ruby is not investing her time helping people heal and feel their best through massage therapy and energy healings, she is wearing her mom hat and sharing her love, energy, and attention to her two young, beautiful and energetic boys.

Her message to the world is to love yourself and invest in your well-being. After all, we are the most important person in our lives and should start treating ourselves that way...right now!

Ruby Botello
massageevolved@gmail.com
(312) 818-1901

Amanda Racheal Sanchez

"We may have ideas and plans for our life, but God has a greater purpose."

How often have we thought of all the things we want to do and accomplish in life? Growing up, most little girls want to be a princess. We envision the big beautiful dresses, the large mansions and castles, and of course, our Prince Charming. Our imagination, dreams, and aspirations are very lofty when we're children. What happens when life unfolds and "reality" sets in? What happens when those dreams don't come true?

GROWN TOO SOON

One night I woke up lost and confused. "Where's my mom?" I thought. As I looked up, I noticed her across the dark room. I quietly called out to her, but she did not respond. I got up to go see her.

With a tremble in my voice I call out, "Mom?" "What are you doing here?"

"Go to bed!" she yelled. I found her standing next to a tall dresser slightly hunched over, straw in hand and nose. I ran to bed crying, wondering why my mom was doing drugs. I was only five years old. What does a five-year-old know about drugs? This was my first encounter with drugs and it certainly wasn't my last.

I grew up in an unstable environment where I was continually built up and broken down. Drugs and alcohol made way for emotional, mental, and physical abuse. Both my parents had no control when emotions ran high. As the oldest child, it was my responsibility to protect my younger sister and brother. I tried my best to shield them from witnessing the abuse.

One night when I was in eighth grade, my father came home looking and sounding like the Hulk. He and my mom were yelling at each other at the top of their lungs. Things quickly turned physical. As always, I was yelling for them to stop and telling him to just leave. My six-year-old brother came out of his room and pulled on my dad's arm to get him away from my mom. In a rage, my dad pulled his hand away and pushed my brother into the wall.

My father had never laid a hand on us. I knew something was really wrong. "Stay here with Megan and hide under the covers! Don't come out, ok?" I told my brother as I put him in the room.

Our all white bathroom had a beautiful vintage, oval, porcelain tub. It was the most beautiful thing we owned. My parents were in there and when I entered to separate them, the room looked like a horror scene. There was nothing but blood splattered EVERYWHERE! I panicked as I thought he was killing my mother! I don't remember how, but they broke apart, and he ran out. Shaking and trembling from head to toe, my mom tried to console me. "Calm down, calm down!" she said. "It's not my blood."

One night, sometime later, I was abruptly awakened from my sleep. "Get up! Hurry! We have to leave before he comes back!" All I could remember was how afraid I felt as my mother rushed me, my brother, and my sister out of the house! All we had with us was a large comforter as we ran out and away from the man my mother thought wanted to kill her. We moved so fast that we didn't really have time to think, just to act. I remember running as fast as we could through the dark streets of Logan Square, stopping in the playground to sleep for a moment because we just couldn't run anymore. I was so afraid and worried someone would find us and hurt us.

Years later, I came home to my mother who was under the influence of drugs and in a suicidal rage.

"Give me $20!" she repeatedly said as we were standing outside on our third-floor porch.

"No. I don't have any money."

"Yes, you do, and you better give it to me, or I'll jump." My mom proceeded to climb over the railing and stand on the three-inch ledge. "Give it to me now or I'll let go!"

I yelled for my dad. I didn't know what to do. I instinctively grabbed my mom like a rag doll and threw her down onto the porch. The look in her eyes and the smirk on her face as she chuckled haunts me to this day. It was as if she was possessed. She wanted to kill us both. This was my life at age 22.

FINDING COMFORT

Why do I share these stories? Because that was my normal life. I never planned for it, but I had to quickly grow up and be the responsible "adult" in order to raise my siblings and my parents. I developed major trust issues because of the mental and emotional damage from my home environment. I always thought to myself that I didn't need anyone else and I could take care of things on my own. I did take care of my family after all, so what could someone else really do for me?

When I wanted the attention and affection I wasn't receiving at home, I turned to all the wrong guys. Guys who didn't care but were always after one thing and got mad when they didn't get it. I never learned how to develop healthy relationships with guys and in turn had low standards.

My outlet from the dramatic reality I called life was school. I became a perfectionist, so I could control everything I could. If I did, I knew everything would be right. I excelled academically and delved head first into extracurricular activities, often being in four or more given activities at once. I took on whatever would keep me away from home and it all had a purpose and impact in my life.

Most notable was the TRiO Upward Bound program. It was through this program that my exploration of a world outside of Chicago really began. I had strong mentors, father figures, and an unbelievable support network that helped cultivate my character into the woman that I am today. I was blessed to travel across the country to more than twenty states and two countries

(Canada and Mexico) in 3-1/2 years for FREE! We visited numerous universities, historical sites, and had an array of cultural explorations. If it wasn't for this program, I may have never really known of the world outside my home and would not have developed my love for travel.

International travel was always a dream! I never thought it would be possible as I never had the money, but with hard work, support and a blessing from God, I was able to study abroad in Barcelona, Spain. I won the grand prize of $10,000 for the DeVry University and MiGente.com's essay contest, *"MiGente con Mente."* We had to write about why education was important in the Latino community. I noted that "our ancestors fought hardships every day of their lives so we may see a brighter future tomorrow. We Latinos need to pay back our families, not with money, but with love, respect, and knowledge to embrace and take charge of our future." I was determined to take full advantage of what had been given to me so that I could give back to others.

My greatest influencer, my anchor, my rock, my foundation was my *abuela* (grandmother). Outside of school, she was the solitude in my life. Whatever I needed, she provided. Whenever I needed her, she was there. She was my hero. She was like my mom.

She helped my mom raise me. She never liked my home situation and would save me from it and distract me as much as she could. I had a great relationship with my abuela! She taught me independence, faith, strength, hustle, entrepreneurship (before I even knew what that was), how to care for a family, and how to care for yourself. I turned to Abuela for everything in life. I knew her words and guidance could be trusted. She never let me down.

When I was three or four years old, I remember telling her "Abuela, we're going to die together when we're 100 years old." Sadly, not only was that impossible, but it certainly wasn't the case when I was 27 years old.

My grandmother suffered from a tumor in her abdomen that wrapped around and crushed her spine. I remember the final night she was home. She was a stubborn woman who refused to go to the hospital. I could still hear the screaming and weeping all night long as she tried to adjust. At one point, she asked me to help her up and the scream she let out because of the pain crushed my soul! I was devastated to hear and see the strongest woman I have ever known be at the weakest moment in her life, and there was nothing I could do to take her pain away. She was admitted to the hospital the next morning and diagnosed with Non-Hodgkin's Lymphoma. She put up a good fight, but three months later, she passed away.

THE PATH TO REDEMPTION

My world was crushed. The one thing to stand true in my life was now taken away. Where was I to go? Who was I to turn to? Thankfully, my grandmother was a woman of God who instilled faith in me from the day I was born. I was on a newfound journey to find out who this Jesus Christ was that she taught me about.

I knew him as a religious character in a story, but I didn't have a personal relationship with Him. I longed to be a follower of Christ, not a fake Christian who did mere traditional acts of worship. I wanted to know this Lord and Savior. I wanted to authentically and wholeheartedly follow Christ, to be obedient to the life he called me to live, the one my grandmother always told me about. With the love, patience, and guidance of my newfound church family, I learned who Christ really was and how he loved and valued me so much. I learned how he deemed me worthy. He had forgiven me of all the pain I had caused in my life of seeking attention and perfection. It is with His love that I found my value, my worth, my significance, and my purpose. Christ was my true rock and foundation. He was the anchor of my hope.

Despite all the pain I have endured in my life, I know there is one thing that is true. God did not have me go through it all for nothing. As my mentor, Matt Sapaula, often says, "Things don't happen to you, they happen for you." If it had not been for my struggles, I would not have a strong character. I wouldn't know how to withstand the storms of life. I may have not developed the appetite for travel and known its delicious taste. Most importantly, I would not have turned to Jesus the way I had and given my life to follow his purpose for me.

There is purpose in the pain. My purpose now is to show women that there is not only a way to survive, but to thrive and push past the pain. I get to impact the lives of so many by sharing this story. Being vulnerable is never easy, but it is so freeing. God has always wanted me to share my story but I've been fearful to do so. I pray that it has blessed you and inspired you.

Remember, we may have ideas and plans for our life, but God has a greater purpose and may take you in a different direction. Know that "when your plans align with God's plans, you're a force to be reckoned with." (Pastor Eddie Leon of Citylights Church). Or as it says in the Bible, *"A person's heart plans his ways, but the Lord determines his steps."* - Proverbs 16:9

REFLECTION

1. What dreams have you let go because life got too hard and too busy?

2. What can you do today to start dreaming again and live out that dream?

3. Do you believe "life doesn't happen to you... it happens for you?" How can you shift your perspective?

BIOGRAPHY

Amanda Racheal Sanchez is a follower of Christ who has always had a mission to impact the lives of those around her. She is a loving wife, daughter, aunt, friend and bonus mom to three teens, Ivan, Jeremiah, and Eliana. To see her in her happiest state, you'll have to see her dancing!

She received her B.A. in Psychology in 2009 from Aurora University in hopes of becoming a child psychologist. In 2015, she became a licensed life insurance and financial professional.

Amanda and her husband, Felix, run a financial firm that educates minority and middle class families on financial concepts typically reserved for the wealthy, educating them about preserving their family's financial dignity, independence, and leaving a legacy.

Amanda is also the founder of Queens Redeemed. She seeks to empower women, their businesses, and their finances by sharing stories of fellow female entrepreneurs, helping promote their businesses, and establishing financial fortitude. Amanda believes every Queen has a story to tell. We never know who we may encourage by sharing it.

She also mentors women in taking a leap of faith and walking into entrepreneurship. Success does not happen overnight, but step-by-step. With perseverance and passion, it can happen.

Amanda Racheal Sanchez
QueensRedeemed@gmail.com
(312) 870-0810

169

PRAYING, TRUSTING, AND BELIEVING

Chanabelle Arriaga

"Every mountain teaches you how to climb the next one."

The moment that you "get it," all the signs, words of encouragement, and conversations finally click and you ask yourself, *why did it take so long?* It took me 48 years to recognize that every mountain I climbed taught me a lesson that would guide me up the next one.

FIRST MOUNTAINS

Everyone called my parents Doña Nidia and Don Manolo. They were much older than my friend's parents and sometimes mistaken for our grandparents.

Growing up in Corona, Queens, my sister Denise and I embraced and enjoyed the life our parents provided. Dad worked at Jacobi Medical Center and mom was a private nurse. As Elders at our church, Centro Biblico, they created another family for us that would be with us throughout our lives.

Dad was well-respected and mom was the caretaker to as many as she could fit under her wings. Meanwhile, Dad was very strict and reserved, but Mami showed us how to love unconditionally. Denise was quiet and sweet and I was daring and mischievous. We were each other's keeper!

In 1986, we visited our brother, Jose "Chema" Reinoso and his family, who had just moved about 3-1/2 hours away to Lancaster, Pennsylvania. Chema is the Spanish voice of Dr. Charles Stanley with In Touch Ministries. This ministry provided our brother and his family the opportunity to travel the world and share the gospel. Soon after, I moved in with my brother and his family, which prompted my parents and sister to also relocate to Pennsylvania.

GOD'S GRACE AND LOVE

Being the new girl in high school was not fun. I was very different and stood out from the others. I dated one of the school jocks, and it wasn't long before he wanted to have sex. I was a virgin and not ready, so we broke things off. So then I dated a guy that had been pursuing me and after our second time, I was pregnant! I hid it from my parents for about three months. When I told my mother, she was heartbroken and cried endlessly, especially since she herself was a virgin until she was 49. It was too much to bear, and my parents had me go live with a close family friend. *This was God showing me Grace.*

My son Michael was born a preemie weighing three pounds, four ounces. I became scared when I realized *this was now my life.* I had made this choice! For three months, I visited my son in the hospital daily and worked part-time. Soon after Michael arrived home, Mami had a stroke! I remember asking God what was happening with my life. I was 16 with a baby and now my guide, my strength, my protector, our mom was on her death bed. We thought she wasn't going to make it, but God heard our prayers. However, when she came home, she didn't recognize us and *this mountain seemed impossible to climb!* She had always been fearless, strong, and caring to everyone around her. So my sister and I followed her example and cared for her, our dad, and Michael.

While mom's health progressed, I was excelling in school and work. My son and I lived in a shelter which provided structure and guidance. They gave me the opportunity to learn a trade and I became a certified medical assistant.

Did I mention I was one of the first students to become pregnant at my high school? My most embarrassing moment prompted them to open a day care in the school, enabling all teen mothers to graduate. *This was God showing me Love.*

CHOICES AND CONSEQUENCES

While living in Lancaster, I met a gentleman named Aaron who gave me my first job and taught me some valuable lessons in life. He believed in me when nobody else did. He made sure Michael had formula and diapers. Aaron's investment in me would impact my life forever. Denise and her best friend Tammy also stood by me through thick and thin. They all taught me valuable lessons and I have lived my life "paying it forward."

On Mother's Day, 1991, I got a call that one of my best friends, Leo, had passed away. Leo and I met at Mount Lawn Camp when I was five and we become instant brother and sister. Losing him changed my life!

Leo had a younger brother named Billy who avoided me all those years we went to camp. He would ask his mom to tell me he wasn't home when I would call for Leo. But as life happened, Billy and I connected after Leo's passing. He was in the Marine Corps and would drive from Camp Lejeune, North Carolina to Lancaster to visit Michael and me. In our pain, we got to know one another and together, we learned to deal with Leo's absence!

In June, I had the opportunity to leave the unhealthy relationship I was in and start fresh. My parents made it very clear their home did not have a revolving door. So if I left, there was no turning back. I packed our bags and the Bronx became our new home. Billy's parents embraced Michael with all the love they had left in them because he was, in some way, part of their healing. I expected smooth sailing and a warm welcome but found choppy, unaffectionate waters. Sadness and pain resonated throughout the house, but Bill and I wanted to honor our love and we got married in February of 1994.

That December, we welcomed our daughter and named her Leah (after Leo). When Leah was about four years old, she noticed her name was in her brother *Michael's* name. I felt it was a sign that Bill and I were meant to be together.

As a family, we agreed to invest the money from Leo's passing and open a Spanish restaurant, El Coqui on Castle Hill. My father-in-law and husband ran the business and I worked as a medical assistant up until 2001, when I started working at Plaza Construction. This is where I grew from a young, timid girl to an outgoing and fearless executive assistant.

I worked with incredible and not so nice people. I had the privilege of working for the Fisher family and Richard Wood. I became one of the top executive assistants and acquired what seemed to be the "perfect life." I thought having my nails and hair done and being the best dressed was important. I attended church and was a mentor with Heavenbound 7, based out of a Christian skateboard shop, where I volunteered with underprivileged young men and women. As a family, we loved volunteering with Hope for the Warriors and caring for our wounded veterans.

From the outside everything looked great, but behind the scenes, I was neglecting my husband, spoiling my kids and trying to keep up a lifestyle that was not my own. They say "you live and you learn" but *we don't all learn right away.*

I filled my void doing good for others. I bought and gave as much as I could because it made me happy to see others happy. Yet ultimately, I still wasn't happy. Living to make others happy backfired and cost a very dear family member to walk away. It left a void that has impacted the last seven years of our lives and those around us. Truly our choices come with consequences and eventually, bring an awareness that things need to change.

INVESTING IN ME

On my 15th anniversary at Plaza Construction, I made the tough decision to resign. The next day I went on my first hike and started to learn about myself. I found inspiration from artist Shantell Martin, who encourages us to search within and love ourselves by asking: who am I? Once I asked myself this question, life changed.

A trusted friend offered me what I thought was an amazing opportunity as a house manager/personal assistant. The job was difficult at first but I gave it my all and began seeing the hard work pay off. Three months later, I was let go! *I saw this as another mountain in my way, but every mountain teaches you how to climb the next one.* The dismissal enabled me to prepare for November when we lost our beautiful home in Fair Lawn, New Jersey.

We were forced to move back to the Bronx. My husband and I had worked so hard to live that American Dream that being back in the Bronx felt unbearable at times. But it has been in that discomfort and pain that God has been showing us His purpose for our lives.

In 2016 I chose to invest in myself! Unemployed and unfulfilled with life, I met with a friend Lexi, who had been attending women empowerment workshops. She encouraged me to invest in myself and seek my purpose.

Once again, my husband was supportive of me doing what made me happy. That October, he gifted me the opportunity to attend a women's summit with the Business of WE, which stands for women entrepreneurs. That room was full of power, confidence, humility, authenticity, unity, and the passion that I sought. I signed up for workshops, seminars, women's conferences at different churches, and started to develop relationships with influencers and women living their purpose.

Just when I thought all was well, my best friend passed in April 2017 and mom died three months later. Life turned upside down and once again it felt like I was taking two steps forward and ten steps back.

This was one of *the biggest mountains in my journey!* I went through a bad depression and couldn't seem to climb out of this dark, uncomfortable place. Smoking numbed the pain. What did it matter? I lost my mom, the one who loved and understood me like no other. It took a trip to Florida on the one-year anniversary of her death for me to "get it!" My sister was in my face and made it clear that failing was not an option and I needed to get it together and live the life God intended for me. Thank you, Denise!

EVERYTHING that I had experienced was part of my story. I was supposed to experience the pain, loss, betrayal, and doubt throughout my life because it was all developing the woman God had created me to be.

I had been doing things "Chanabelle's way." I had to "let go and let God." I now had to give up the control I was so used to having and allow my husband to care for me. Letting go was the key to a love and appreciation I had never felt before. I embraced humility and learned that "less is more!" Letting go of the fear and forgiving myself is liberating. I began to love me for who I was and seek God more.

I am now in a place of "Wow!" My husband and I have never been so in tune with one another. I am surrendering it all and now live my life seeking God's will and living a purpose-filled life.

Launching my business in 2019 will be a demonstration of faith and the life God had planned for me and my family all along. I am excited and look forward to sharing His love with you. As my sister said, "Life isn't about waiting for the storm to pass… it's learning to dance in the rain."

Thank you to those who have stood by me, prayed for me, supported me and made this all possible. There are so many of you who have touched my heart. I recognize that everyone has a purpose in life, whether for a season or a lifetime.

This story is dedicated to my mother and my husband.

REFLECTION

1. What mountains are you facing? How are you overcoming them?
2. Are you afraid of failing? Don't be, YOU CAN DO THIS!
3. Do you believe your prayers are answered? Even when things get difficult?

BIOGRAPHY

Chanabelle Arriaga is the Founder of In-Serenity. In October of 2018, she took a leap of faith and began to create a business that would inspire and empower all who connect with her. Chanabelle's passion for home and office organization is a gift she wants to share with others and she has begun creating gift of love and personalized gifts as a way of revealing God's love for all.

She has worked as an Executive Assistant/Office Manager for large corporations/foundations. As a strong leader, she is dedicated to be the change and spread love and happiness! Chanabelle has a commitment to support organizations such as Combat to Veterans, Heavenbound 7, Hope for the Warriors, ICLA Foundation, Overcoming Toxic Emotions, and Project ALS.

In 2015, she was recognized by the United States Marine Corps Barracks in Washington D.C. for her volunteer services. She is on the Community Connections for Youth Board and is an active member at Harvest Fields Community Church.

Chanabelle and her husband now hike together and look forward to climbing the highest mountains. Her days are spent creating, motivating, and becoming the woman God has called her to be. She aspires to inspire by sharing her story.

Chanabelle Arriaga
chanabelle@in-serenity.com
(917) 882-3095

Tanya Flores

"The Universe is with you and it always has your back."

You were divinely created, just like a snowflake. It's very unlikely there is anyone exactly like you in the world. Your story, your experiences, personality, and choices shape the extraordinary human being that you are!

Women have been the main mentors in my life; my grandmother, mother, and aunts became extended mothers to me. My grandmother stayed at home and raised 15 children. My grandfather ran a trucking business and distributed construction materials, but when my mom was only nine years old, he died of a stroke. My grandma was left to raise them all. She lived in a rural town in Mexico where employment opportunities were limited for a woman needing to support a large family.

Eventually, my grandmother immigrated to the United States and took a job cleaning at Cabrini Green Hospital in Chicago. Like many immigrants, she sent the money she made back to her country to feed her children. She didn't crumble during this challenge. I come from a line of warrior women, and this has taught me that everyone has the power to pull themselves up when they get hit hard in life. This power can propel you to build big dreams.

MY VOICE

I was born in Chicago's Cook County Hospital, a nine-pound, chubby baby. My mom immigrated here as a single mom without a college education. She worked in many physically demanding, factory jobs for little pay. She also raised my sister, Leanett, and my brother, Julio. After my parent's divorce, Julio went to live with his dad. I was in high school when they split up, and she bought a used trailer park home. It had brown, metal siding and a little outdoor shed. She made just enough to get by, making sure she was always home to take care of us when we got out of school. I saw my mom struggle, and I felt deep down that God was calling me to be more. The Universe is always calling you to be more. As Kahlil Gibran said in his book, *The Prophet*, "Children are life's longing for itself."

You were born into this world with a very special and unique purpose. Once you discover it, you can share it all with the world. That's why taking the time to listen to your inner voice is so key. Your life may be difficult on the outside, but there is a positive light, stronger than anything, inside you. This optimism can turn everything around!

I began to search for my voice. I joined youth groups in my church and Hispanic Leadership groups at my school. Oddly enough, I was drawn to speech team. I used to be so shy and embarrassed standing in front of people that I'd turn bright red as a tomato and want to hide. But I knew that if I joined, I could improve my public speaking. I wanted to fit in with my friends, but when I asked them to join me, they all said no. It almost held me back, but at the age of 15, I took the plunge and joined the team. Right then and there, I decided that if I had a dream to pursue, it was all up to me. A dream is only yours and yours alone. You can't expect others to have that yearning desire in their soul as you do! The only person that can say no to your dream is YOU! Certainly, nobody will pay the consequences for your choices, so you might as well choose what feels right for you.

After graduating from high school, I enrolled at DePaul University and graduated with a B.A. with double concentrations in Human Development and Commercial Spanish. Meanwhile, I also earned my real estate license, but entered the profession just as the market crashed.

Still, I had my degree and was ready to conquer the world. I went to apply for a job at a nonprofit organization, but the pay was low, not even a livable wage, and I was now supporting my sister as well as myself. I saw an ad for a position at JP Morgan Chase and applied there. They paid twice as much, and I could still help people. It was a job, but not my lifelong dream.

THE ROAD TO OUR DREAMS

Dreams are also built in life changing moments. One of these happened just three years ago. My husband and I were in the middle of building a wonderful life together. He had written an award-winning book on marketing and had created a very successful global sales training program for entrepreneurs. I was leading my online marketing and print business and had just curated and presented an event, TedXPilsenWomen, which had been a dream of mine for some time.

That morning, I asked him if he could take the girls to daycare so I could finish up the event. He said he'd take a shower first. I helped my two and four-year-old daughters get ready, walked into the bathroom to wash my hands, and found my husband lying flat on the floor. I said, "Carlos, Carlos…" He was mumbling and unable to utter a word.

I picked up the phone and calmly called 911, never even processing how much our life was about to change. Within minutes, I heard a siren and saw a fire truck with the number "5" on it pull up our driveway. Six muscular firemen walked through my door. They said, "Come on, man, get up." But Carlos couldn't get up. They carried him out of the house, into the ambulance, and took him to Mt. Sinai hospital. I was told that they were unable to help him, and he needed to be transferred to Rush Hospital.

I carried on my day as normally as I could, communicating with our virtual business team of seven to let them know my husband had just suffered a stroke. I took my girls to daycare, trying not to disrupt their lives even more.

He stayed there for a month. During the day, his mom stayed with him while I continued to run the business. He was unable to move for days. The doctors said he had developed aphasia, and it would take time to recover his reading, writing, and speaking ability. In one morning, my life had completely changed. As I walked through the corridors of the hospital, I felt that a Phoenix was being born, giving me the strength to rise from these ashes and survive whatever came my way.

My husband's stroke was a life-altering event. Others regard it as a tragedy, but I don't, because from the moment I found him on the ground, I knew he'd be okay. I have become a stronger woman, but it was challenging for my family to adjust. I lost the man I married and enjoyed in conversation. Our family needed to create a new relationship with him, post-stroke, with no language skills.

Life can change for you in the blink of an eye and if you lose your optimism and hope, you've lost it all. That is the biggest threat to your dreams. I have been there before; I've let other people's fears into the realm of my dreams.

Here's my belief that I wish to pass on to you: The Universe is with you and it always has your back.

The day of the stroke, the fire truck was the number 5 and his hospital room was the number 5. That number always had a magical presence in my life. That day God spoke to me, letting me know that all would be well.

Carlos had a community of more than 25,000 subscribers and had coached over 100 students. He had been in the middle of coaching a sales mastery class before the stroke, so at first, I took over the instruction. I didn't want to alarm the students, so I just told them Carlos could not be there. Meanwhile, our team worked harder than ever to keep the sales coaching business growing.

My husband returned home, not yet recovered, but at least alive. We all have challenging times in our lives; the key is to not lose faith but believe. You must keep moving forward! We continued to grow and created more than 100 new videos and trained thousands of entrepreneurs through virtual webinars. Our registrations skyrocketed.

A NEW DREAM FOUND

I enjoyed coaching entrepreneurs and sales professionals very much! I enjoyed seeing them regain their confidence and I personally coached more than 100 entrepreneurs.

My husband was getting better, and he could communicate a little bit more. However, in his search for new meaning, deep down I don't think he thought it was fair that I was running his baby, the business.

With the help of my beautiful friend and team member Natalia, I think we were on the cusp of evolving the business to new heights, but instead, I let that energy get away from me because I didn't want conflict with my husband. He may tell you another version of this story. In life, everyone has a different version, so instead of fighting for where I believed Academia Triunfadores was going, I decided to get back into real estate, which is something I knew I could do outside of the corporate world. After all, it was our four-unit building in Pilsen where we lived in that made the bump in my life easier. We sold the property and paid off our debts. We invested in a smaller home to fix and flip.

Building your dreams starts with believing and knowing you deserve to create anything you want. In 2018 after my husband's stroke, I created Darloop Group. We got into real estate investing.

I also created a group called Chicas Real Estate, and I run a wellness and health business with Arbonne. Everything I do on TanyaFores.tv is focused on helping others build their dreams.

REFLECTION

1. The biggest regret on your deathbed will be what you didn't do. If you were on your deathbed today, what would that regret be?

2. Dreams come as a spark of inspiration. What is one dream/goal that keeps showing up for you, but you haven't yet accomplished? What small step can you take to achieve it?

3. What negative experience have you had in the past that you can use for good in the future?

BIOGRAPHY

Tanya Flores is a Chicago-based, real estate agent with eXp Realty and an investor with Darloop Group. She's been a renter, a landlord, and has also flipped houses as a real estate investor and agent. Tanya is a graduate of DePaul University, is certified in real estate negotiation, and has completed coursework to become a certified property pricing advisor. She is also the founder of Chicas Real Estate, a space created for women in the real estate industry to help them grow their businesses and personally succeed. She hosts the show, *We Love This City*, which is produced by her husband, through their company, Darloop Media Inc.

Tanya is a multi-passionate entrepreneur and a coach and trainer with Academia Triunfadores, a community of over 100,000 entrepreneurs that her husband created. She produces inspirational content to encourage others to build their dreams. She also has a healthy living business with Arbonne, the number one company for healthy living inside and out, which helps women create better health and financial futures for their loved ones.

Tanya Flores
contact@tanyaflores.net
(773) 234-0822

Chella Diaz

"You are the boss…money is your employee."

I have wonderful memories of being an adventurous young girl growing up in a town outside of Guadalajara. When I was nine years old I would go to the fruit and vegetable stands in the Mercado. The first thing I would look for was the seller with the biggest, ripest tomatoes and then I could begin my shopping.

The stands seemed so big. I was small and couldn't hand money over the counter so I would go into the stall next to the mountain of produce and pay there. My parents left money in a jar on our kitchen table. There were always a few coins left over I could save, giving me an appreciation for the value of money which would later lead to helping me purchase my first car at 17 years old. Later that year, we would move to the U.S. and settle in California.

THE SPIRITUAL JOURNEY BEGINS

While growing up in Southern California, I led a very sheltered life. Although there were always people around me, I felt empty and alone. Something was missing and there was a void I needed to fill.

In my early twenties I met the man that would become my husband. I had my first son, got married and had my second son. I was married for 17 years and then divorced.

That's when my spiritual journey began. I started taking yoga classes, which encouraged me to become a Kundalini Yoga teacher. I continued to learn, expanding my mind by taking courses in Theta Healing and Reiki. I became a Reiki Master and teacher, still seeking to fill that emptiness. Reiki was the first step in allowing me to heal, releasing some of my early baggage.

I continued learning through courses, workshops and networking groups. In one year I spent 165 days in workshops and trainings. I was determined to fill my void. I spent a lot of money, chased shiny objects, worked with several coaches, and learned a great deal in the process.

In September of 2017 I received a Starlight Attunement; the self-healing continued. Then, with a feeling that I was being channeled by a dream, I was guided to move to Portland, Oregon in April 2018. I had never been there. However, the pull was so strong I followed it. So in May 2018, I packed my car and drove to Oregon. The minute I crossed the border I felt at peace. The tall green trees and brightly colored flowers were like nothing I had ever seen before. Even the rest areas were special; clean and spacious. I spent time at rest areas journaling and taking in my surroundings.

I reached out to a few folks asking for suggestions on what cities would be best to find a place to live since the living arrangements I had made had fallen apart. I found myself wondering if I had made a mistake. I stayed several nights in hotels and felt very vulnerable carrying all my belongings in the car. I felt lost, living out of a suitcase.

THE PORTLAND TRANSFORMATION

In May, a friend from Florida moved to Seattle and offered me a place to stay until I figured things out. Two weeks later, I traveled to Milwaukie, Oregon. I met and stayed with a woman who had a business helping baby boomers with large homes find roommates. Within a few days, I had found and moved into my new home.

The month of June was a whirlwind. I moved into my residence. Days later I attended my first networking event and found a client. A week later, I hosted a "Transcend Abundance Event" for 23 women. Then I volunteered for the World Domination Summit Event and on the 29th, I rented space at a wellness center.

Between June and July of 2018, I received three 7th Dimension Attunements which fused all the healing modalities I had been exploring for the past 15 years, tying them together in a Tiffany box with a big silver ribbon. I could no longer hide from the work I was born to do.

During my three months in Portland I became a new person. Perhaps that was why I was guided there. I felt as if I had shed many layers of baggage overnight. My morning routines were solid. I wouldn't start the day without doing my meditations. I was open to new adventures and I asked for guidance; people with the answers showed up. I was changing so fast, meeting amazing people and I soon built a supportive community. I was one of a few Latinas in the area and I searched for community events, especially live music performances which are my favorite.

Portland has an amazing public transportation system. The train was just a ten- minute walk from my house and allowed me to explore my new environment. I could take four main trains to reach the different neighborhoods and all the majesty offered there. I had a great time. I was that little girl again from Juchitlan on an adventure. I was meeting people and asking for help. This was a big step; in the past, I had never asked for help. Now, I was ready to open myself up to receive.

I don't want to give you the wrong impression. I did encounter some prejudiced people along the way, but now I reacted differently. There was a profound change in me. I realized people are entitled to their opinions. They were reacting from the prejudices and ignorance of their raising. I didn't have to take their comments personally.

The person I was becoming was what mattered. I was seeing love in everyone and appreciated their journey. It's about how we choose to react to people. We can allow them to take us to their level or we can shine our light so brightly we will attract the right people. The people that should not be in our lives will leave. Just imagine if you started to see everyone as pure love. Life would become much easier and joyful.

A FINANCIAL FORMULA

I would like to share a few things to help you on your journey to more peace and joy.

1. **Take inventory of where you are and where you want to go.** Be honest. Put all your cards on the table without judgment. This step will get you on your ideal track. I make lists to keep up with the things I want to accomplish. Start with your ultimate goal in mind, for example, paying off debt. What is the balance? What is your current payment? How much do you need to pay monthly in order to pay off the loan in your desired time frame? Or, you may want to save three months of your monthly obligations. How much do you need to save each week/month to accomplish that goal?

2. **Keep track of every dollar you spend.** This is the magic formula that has been proven to work for my clients. Any time you spend more than a dollar write it down. At the end of the week, divide what you spend into two columns: "wants" and "needs." Do this for a total of four weeks. You simply make the list; no judgments or changes. After four weeks, you will have the magic formula. Your "needs" list is what I need to meet your monthly obligations (mortgage/rent, phone bill, groceries, etc.). The "wants" list is where you make different choices to save money.

3. **Put your money into three different buckets:** (1) Needs, (2) Wants and (3) Possibility. Your first concern are your monthly obligations. The second includes how much you spend on movies, dining out, etc. and the third is the possibility bucket. This is where you save for three months of monthly obligations, vacations, new tires, auto repairs, investments, etc. This is where the magic happens. You can start with one account. As it builds, open a second account. I recommend you open your possibility account with a different institution from your regular account. A portion of your monthly wages could go into the account automatically. This is one of the best ways to stay on track and watch your account grow. Soon you will find it easier to say no to temptations, i.e. you're too tired to cook, so you go out to eat. Instead, you could prepare a few meals in advance and freeze them and you will always have meals ready.

4. **Get Creative.** If you're looking at what you want to accomplish and feel a little discouraged, now is the time to think outside of the box. Take on a short-term job adding income to reach your goal more quickly. Could you sell anything you're no longer using? One client started brewing her coffee and only went out to lunch on payday instead of every Friday. She was able to pay off three credit cards and build a savings.

5. **Next, list at least five rewards you will give yourself when you accomplish a milestone.** List ideas include: manicures/pedicures, a car wash, a drive to the beach/mountains, a nice lunch/dinner.

6. **Create a pride/success/ got-it-done wall.** Use colored paper and different color post-its. Anytime you do something you are proud of write it down and post-it to your wall. This comes in handy when you're having a low day because it reminds you to stay on track. At a glance, you will see proof of all you've accomplished.

7. **A morning routine builds a healthy and abundant life.** Studies show people who accomplish the most have a consistent morning ritual. I encourage you to find yours. What are the things you can do to prepare yourself for a successful day? Some people read, others meditate, work out, and walk. As I mentioned before, doing a meditation and asking for guidance is a must for me. I ask for help staying grounded so that I see the opportunities in front of me, see people for who/what they are and to help me come from pure love. I continue to work on "judgment." I tend to jump to conclusions, letting my ego take the driver's seat. Now when I'm ready to jump to conclusions I take a few deep breaths and ask myself why I am being triggered. Silently I say, "I love you, I love you" to the other person, then to

myself. This grounds me again and brings a great deal of joy. Of course this does not mean that I want to be around negative people; it's just a way for me to have compassion for their journey. Who knows what type of life the person has?

These steps will help you accomplish your financial goals. Have compassion for yourself when you start. Know that things and people are going to test you. It is okay to get off track. It's not about how many times you get off track, but how many times you get back on track to attain your goals.

You are the boss…money is your employee.

Take a little ride with me. Imagine you've paid off your debt and have three months of monthly obligations in an account. You've received a raise/bonus at work. You put a portion of the additional money into your possibility account. There's less stress and more time on your hands. You're no longer working the part-time job. You're looking for ways to give back. You volunteer at a school, thrift store, pet shelter, community center and find that this brings much joy. You meet new people and learn so many things.

Once my kids were out of school, I volunteered at a thrift shop. I did this for eight years. I met interesting people and learned so much. Something magical happens when you share a common purpose. There's an instant bond.

My journey is far from over. I live with joy and a sense of adventure, just as I did when I was a young girl.

REFLECTION

1. What are you journeying towards?

2. Is money your boss or employee? Do you need to make a change?

3. Which of the seven steps can you enact today to help you achieve your financial goals?

BIOGRAPHY

Chella knew at a very young age she was different from the other kids. She was able to see and feel things other kids could not. She didn't want to stand out so she put her gifts to sleep.

For more than 10 years, Chella has been on her spiritual journey. She was married for 17 years and has two sons.

Her list of completed certifications and programs is quite extensive but includes Reiki Master, Reiki Teacher, Starlight Energy and her most recent, which brought all her certifications together in a powerful way, 7th Dimension Healing Energy.

As a vessel for 7th Dimension Healing Energy, Chella meets every client where they are and provides the tools they need to get them to where they want to go. She has been hosting workshops for women to help them master their money skills.

Chella Diaz
moneymap101@gmail.com
www.chelladiaz.com

Fernanda Arteaga

"It's our mistakes that lead to our self-improvement."

I never expected to end up living in the U.S.!

After earning my bachelor's degree in my home country of Venezuela, I was working as an event planner and a freelance writer for *EnBoga* magazine and in a public relations agency, writing press releases for new brand launches such as Ron Veroes, Tarbay, and Lancome.

Several years later, I told my family I wanted to learn English and travel abroad for a cultural exchange program. They asked me to research it carefully and find the best option; they would support my plan.

I found a program through an international school in my country called EF-Education First. They offered me three potential locations to live and study: Vancouver, Canada; Malta, Europe; and Chicago. There was no time to process the VISA for Canada, and Malta was too far from home. I also wondered whether the English speakers in Canada and Europe were as fluent as those in the U.S., and I had heard that the best way to succeed as a young professional was to network with others. There was no better place to do that than in the "Windy City."

So I decided on Chicago and it was the right place for my first experience as an older student. I was happy to find a good school in a city with so much to offer, I was excited to launch my new life in the U.S.!

CHICAGO BEGINNINGS

The Education First program offered an all-inclusive plan. My family paid for my travel to the U.S. and a plan which included accommodations, full-time classes, and two meals a day (breakfast and dinner) for the duration of my ten-month stay. The program helped process my VISA and placed me in a nice home with a wonderful American lady living with her daughter, who was hosting other foreign students like me.

My first night was weird because two of my flights were delayed so I arrived very late. I did not know much English but was excited to learn and had a sense of humor about trying. When I first saw my roommate, I thought she was Asian. She was already asleep, and looked like she had an Asian face. The next morning, I found out she was a Latina from Peru. I was a little disappointed that I would be speaking Spanish with my roommate rather than English, but it was a nice arrangement. Then I met my other roommate who was sleeping in front of us, from Brazil, who spoke Portuguese. Trying to communicate was quite amusing! We lived together for three months. Who would have guessed I would meet people from around the world right in my bedroom?

During my first months in Chicago, I experienced a range of unexpected emotions, all at the same time: awe, sadness, happiness, nervousness, excitement, and fear. I felt like I didn't know what I was doing and missed my family every single day, longing to know my future. This was my first separation from home and close friends. I missed my mom making my meals, caring for me, waiting for me at home to give me a hug when I needed it, and of course, my bed, food, home, car, neighborhood, neighbors, smells of home, and home culture. I missed my dad giving me rides wherever and whenever, and just being happy together, talking and laughing about nothing in particular. I missed my own way of living.

Fortunately, I decided that I had to stop missing everything so much and dedicated all my time to studying, meeting new classmates, and visiting new places.

The days went on, until I met a friend who introduced me to a man from Venezuela who worked for an insurance company. He asked me to help him generate new leads for his business. Technically, it was a part-time job. Thanks to the income, I was able to return to my country for a short, week-long visit with my family. I was going crazy without them!

Many months later, I found a roommate who was from Chile. We still keep in touch to this day. She introduced me to my spiritual coach. Lucy and I hit it off the moment we met. Nowadays, she is my confidant who gives me wonderful guidance about my emotionality, spirituality, love, and relationship with God. She taught me that a strong belief in God leads to good things throughout the universe. At the same time, she reminds me of the saying my grandmother Yolanda taught me: We must serve God to get His blessings. Live by faith.

Like other immigrants, my way has not been easy. We all know that hard work, dedication, responsibility, discipline, confidence, integrity, resilience, perseverance, and creating good habits are some of the values we must keep in mind as we make our way in a new country. To sum it up, hard work is dignity. We must try to do things better every day, with a smile, and keep the desire to keep our dreams alive, day by day and hour by hour. Along the way, we must be conscious of the mistakes we make and make sure we never make them again.

STAYING

In July 2016, the time had come to return home. I had a ticket to fly back to Venezuela, but the country was now in a state of unrest. The economy was in a freefall and inflation was rapidly rising to crisis levels. The everyday economic activity was severely encumbered by a nonsensical system of currency control. People were struggling with hyperinflation, power outages, and terrible food and medicine shortages. It made sense to stay in U.S longer and my family agreed, as did my landlord.

However, my studies were over so my family stopped supporting me financially. Since I wanted to stay, I had to support myself using my meager savings of $500.

I faced a new stage of my life, challenged to live in a new culture with strange people and unpleasant weather. However, I got used to it very quickly. I now like Chicago weather no matter how windy and extremely cold it is. I enjoy it and know how to cope. I quickly learned that the way to save your money is not to spend it on useless things and not to get a loan when you know you cannot repay it. For example, I choose to use public transportation rather than buy a car and make payments. I can use the money I save for groceries and other expenses.

CREATING HOME

To remain in the country legally, I had to continue to study so I found a nice, moderately-priced school and was admitted. But I also needed to work. What could I do? I was still new to the language, but from the start I always tried to meet people, which I found to be very helpful. If you do not talk to others, little will happen. Even though I did not know English well, I tried to immerse myself in the language. My first experience speaking English was as a volunteer for the 2015 Chicago Marathon. I did not care about my fluency because if you want to learn something, you have to make mistakes. It's our mistakes that lead to our self-improvement. Sometimes, it is also good to talk and share your dreams, just in case someone else has the same one and can help you reach yours.

In every new job, I met people who became part of my life and helped me find work in new places. It was a challenge that made me a stronger person. Today, I believe in myself more than ever and am humbler, braver, more grateful and appreciative of things that others have done for me.

I lived with my host family for two years before I was able to move out and live alone. At the age of 30, I found a mortgage lender. I moved again and obtained support from my family to build my little home. I realized that living alone is hard if you are used to living with others. I was now responsible for everything. I learned to cook and discovered the pleasures of preparing food.

I discovered that here in America, "ambition" is a funny thing. You always want more and more, and what you have is never good enough. Living on my own, I began to have a strong drive to succeed. I continued to have adventures. For instance, I had the honor of participating in a few plays and collaborating with others on productions for Chicago radio and TV. In every job I took along the way, I met new people and continued on my journey.

After nearly two years in a business career program, I graduated and the immigration authorities approved me for an OPT (Opportunity Program Training). I needed to find a job within three months. For me, this time was very stressful. I needed to have all the right papers to legally work in the U.S., and I spent time going to many interviews and not finding the right job. Finally, just one day prior to the time I needed to prove employment, I received a call from a man at an employment agency and was placed in customer service at a global insurance provider of supplemental insurance. I could now stay in the country!

I like my new job because it is in a big company with lots of opportunities. Nevertheless, my long-term goals are to develop myself and eventually become licensed in either health, accident, life, car, or real estate. I would also like to become an agent and achieve financial independence. Perhaps I could relocate to work in another state or country. My immediate need is to extend my work permit to continue my employment in the U.S. If this does not work, I will be forced to return to Venezuela. However, I will not stop trying to find a way to stay here. I do not want to waste all the hard work and effort I have put into the last four years.

I still miss my country a lot and have been back twice. Yet I believe that something extraordinary is on the horizon and that's what's keeping me here. Without leaving Venezuela, I could not have worked in restaurants, ice cream stores, as a producer for a media company called "Zu Barrio" and a production assistant with Water People Theater. I've been a biller and salesperson in different car dealerships and now I'm in the insurance industry!

Every step gets better, and if I had to do it all over again knowing how it would turn out, I absolutely would! People make mistakes many times throughout their life. I did too. But my mistakes teach me what needs to be fixed. I have accepted failures and kept on moving. Things can only happen if you try to make them happen. When you get close to your goal, don't give up! Mistakes help us grow as human beings. Also, do not think that nobody will understand if you speak, or that people will laugh at your accent. Speak anyway!

In 2015, everything changed for me when I decided to come to the U.S. I was pretty sure that I was going to be successful in my new life, and I'm slowly but surely making my way! I will not rest until I find happiness doing what I love, finding financial freedom, and bringing my family here to live with me.

REFLECTION

1. What is the last mistake you made? What did you learn?

2. What role does faith play in your life?

3. Have you ever been intimidated by a language barrier? How did you handle it?

BIOGRAPHY

Andrea Fernanda Arteaga Sanabria (a.k.a. Fernanda Arteaga) is a journalist from Caracas, Venezuela who has been living in Chicago for almost four years. She is currently working as a global provider of supplemental insurance, including accident, life, and health insurance with Combined Insurance, a partner of the Chubb Corporation, with locations in North America, Latin America, Europe, and the Pacific.

She is currently single and keeps close ties with her family, including her older brother in Scotland, and her family in Caracas, including her parents, brother, aunts, uncles, nephews, cousins, and especially Mi Tita, who has helped her and her family in everything.

Fernanda is enjoying her journey through life, accompanied by her love of laughter, working hard, and her deep belief and faith in God who helps her along the way. She has a bachelor's degree in journalism from Universidad Santa María in Venezuela and a business career program certificate from the Computer System Institute. She has experience working in event planning, public relations and as a freelance writer for various media outlets.

Fernanda Arteaga
andreaarteaga.aa@gmail.com
(312) 897-0021

Nancy Razón

"You have the power to extinguish the limelight of those who shame."

How many times have you stared at yourself in the mirror and despised yourself and what you saw? How quickly do you judge yourself and find every imperfection on your body? For me, it was too many times.

They say that time is priceless because you can never get it back, yet we use our precious time to shame ourselves. Take a moment to reflect on how shameful this makes you feel. We antagonize ourselves day in and day out, then we put on a facade and go on through our merry day fabricating what we think others might be thinking. Worse yet, we do the same to them, knowing how horrible that feels. I'm guilty.

The reality is that we are not born thinking this way; it's a learned behavior and one we can change. But before we can change anything, we have to take a few minutes to reflect on not only how it makes us feel, but how it all began.

I had never taken the time to think about when "the problem" began for me, not because I didn't have the time, but because I honestly think I didn't want to know. After all, who wants to relive those painful, negative moments?

EARLY SHAME

I do recall feeling ashamed of my body for the first time when I was about 10 years old. I remember being a happy little girl riding my bike around the neighborhood when out of nowhere, I was asked to come inside the house and change my shirt because my flourishing little breasts were visible. I guess I had not really given any thoughts to my body changing at that age. I just wanted to ride my bike, play with my dolls, or play teacher. I do remember feeling very embarrassed and not wanting to ride my bike anymore.

From that moment forward, I became very conscious of my transforming body. I didn't like it. I just wanted to play, but when I was made aware that I was becoming a young lady, it was scary. I didn't know what else was going to happen to my body.

Besides being confused with all the changes going on, now my mom was on my case. "*Mija* (daughter) don't let anyone touch you anywhere! Make sure you don't show!" Oh, I remember how my mom and *tias* (aunts) enjoyed talking about "it." "Did you buy her *corpiño*s (training bras)?" they would ask. I wanted to say to them, why do you have to talk about my boobs like they are some kind of fruit or something? I hated that. Then at school, all the girls were anxiously waiting to grow a pair of their own, as if they were any fun.

By sixth grade I was very aware that my body was not the same as the other girls, and I felt very ashamed. I didn't want anyone to look at me because it was so embarrassing. I remember wearing big shirts because I wanted to camouflage my extras. I was constantly hunching over trying to hide my premature, developing body.

Sixth grade finally came to an end and middle school was about to start. I was finally starting to feel comfortable with my new body, and then one hot summer day, as I went about my business enjoying the weather in my shorts, some girl from my neighborhood asked me if I was going to shave my legs. I was not aware I had to shave my legs for middle school. Was there a list of things I needed to do that nobody gave me?

I immediately went home and told my mom that I had to shave my legs, or all the kids were going to make fun of me and call me spider legs. Being a first-timer, I came out of the shower with many cuts, but it didn't matter. The hairs were gone and I was ready for middle school, or so I thought...

SCHOOL SHAME

My memories of middle school are a big blur. All I recall is that I was a scrawny, brown-skinned girl with boobs that felt out of place. I was always wondering, am I too fat? Am I too tall? Am I too brown? How come everyone else doesn't have boobs? And the list continued...

I was feeding these kind of thoughts to myself daily. Middle schoolers can be cruel and although I didn't personally get shamed by my peers, I was very aware of how others were being humiliated. I felt horrible for them and I stayed quiet because I feared getting the same treatment. I didn't have a strong voice. In fact, I didn't have a voice at all. I was a silent observer trying to save myself from middle school pandemonium.

Thankfully, middle school years passed and I moved on to high school. Oh, the glorious days in high school! So many memories! By then I didn't mind my curves too much; I wanted to to impress the world. I had also found a voice and I wasn't afraid to use it. I became more aware of the shaming many teens received. From weight, to skin color, to clothing, to the brand of shoe you wore, if you had a significant other or not, how you did your hair, who you hung out with, and so on.

Luckily, I always seemed to salvage myself from all that drama. I'm glad I did because I'm sure it would've had a very negative impact on my life, but I always wonder how I managed to do it. I mean, I wasn't the kind of girl that got into fights or tried to intimidate people. But even though I wasn't being shamed, in the back of my mind I was always on my toes. I felt that if I let it slip I would not see the end of it.

Life outside of school was a little different. I felt like my mom was constantly telling me to stop eating so much or be careful about my food choices. I repeatedly overheard my aunts talking to my mom about making sure I didn't overeat because I came from "gente gordita" (fat people). Back then, I was one of the taller girls, and for some reason they seemed to confuse my tallness with being a big girl.

All these overheard conversations made me feel so fat. I was never a slim girl. I'm a Latina with curves. I wear them proudly now, but back then I cannot say the same. I just wanted to be slim like the rest of the girls, but my hips and behind required bigger-sized jeans. That was devastating and I considered it a curse more than a blessing. I now realize that the others longed to have those attributes. Nowadays, everyone is paying to have what I have! Back then it wasn't as popular, or at least in my eyes it wasn't.

FIGHTING SHAME

I never had anyone sit down and explain to me that all body types are different. I just assumed that I was just fat and maybe no one said anything because they were scared of me because I was big and tall.

These kinds of thoughts and side conversations did end up having a detrimental impact on my life. I became very self-conscious of my weight, I hated my body, and it definitely affected my self-esteem in a negative way.

One would wonder, does body shaming still affect today's youth? Unfortunately, more than ever before. Today's youth are bombarded daily with images of what society defines as beautiful in the form of super-skinny female models with perfect skin, makeup, hair, etc. and stunningly handsome, slim or well-built male models with perfect skin, hair and smiles. They portray very unrealistic body types and behaviors that are considered the gold standard in our society. Our youth are striving to follow and become fictional people. Every day they go to school and are harassed by their peers because they don't fit a certain mold that society has painted as the ideal person. This is wrong and we, the adults surrounding them, need to help them realize what really matters. Now that I have grown, matured, and realize what really matters in life and how to love myself, I feel obligated to help youth. There's no reason they should feel any kind of shame. We have to take the time to feed them positive thoughts and give them a safe environment where they can speak freely and ask questions. Think about how many times we had questions that we wouldn't dare ask our mother or father. We wondered but we never had an answer. And if we got an answer, it was most likely from another peer who heard something from an older sibling, cousin, etc.

All my experiences and the magnified shamings that our youth continue to encounter have driven me to dedicate myself to empower their young minds, help them practice self-love, and learn to build each other up. I created a non-for-profit organization, Youth Movement, to better serve the youth in my community. Through the organization, the youth learn leadership skills and are encouraged to become future philanthropists and develop cultural and self-awareness.

In addition, I give conferences about my experiences and create a safe environment where youth open up and speak about their personal experiences. As a result of these encounters I have learned that today's youth deal with a massive amount of idiotic shaming.

SHAMING IN THE DIGITAL WORLD

In the past, you were ridiculed within your school and/or neighborhood, but in today's tech savvy world, you can "go viral" with anything anyone considers a flaw. Millenials have access to technology that amplifies shaming to a new level and could easily ruin someone's life.

Shaming has become such an infectious phenomenon for millennials because of their digital world. Everyone wants to go viral, even at the expense of others. This is called cyberbullying.

Although cyberbullying is more common in teenagers, we can all fall victim. Just last year I was cyberbullied, but because of my personal growth, I was strong enough to keep it from bringing me down. I was also supported by my true friends who chose to take a stand against cyberbullying instead of feeding into the negativity and glorifying the shaming with their likes and shares. We reported the negative comments and had them removed.

We just have to remember our worth and step up our game. Most of the time these bullies want their 15 seconds of fame, but you have the power to extinguish the limelight of those who shame by retracting your likes, comments, and shares, or clicking "report."

We need to teach our youth to use technology in a more positive manner by giving them the tools they need to stop the shaming. In my effort to continue fighting this cause, I have become a mentor to many youth, always hoping to make a difference in their lives by teaching them the dangers of shaming, not only to others, but to themselves as well.

Individuals who have shamed others have lost endorsements, career opportunities and even scholarships because of their choice to deprecate those they consider inferior. Shaming should not be tolerated at any level and if you choose to participate in this crisis, be mindful that the aftermath could have dire consequences. Instead, shine bright like a diamond without dimming anyone's light!

REFLECTION

1. What kind of shaming have you experienced? How did it make you feel and how did you overcome it?
2. How do you motivate yourself when you are feeling down? Do you have a trusted person you can talk to?
3. Have you ever shamed anyone? If so, reflect on that moment. What would you say to that person today?

BIOGRAPHY

Nancy Razón is an educator and civic leader who is passionate about advocating for her community. After receiving her B.A. in Education at Northern Illinois University in 2009, she became a middle school teacher in English Learner (EL) instruction and is now a TPI teacher for the hometown school district.

The philosophies Nancy has learned in education and life experiences have directed her to empower Latino youth in reaching their full potential, achieving educational goals and finding their strengths. Nancy is focused on finding ways to give back to her community, specifically in leading positive development initiatives. She currently serves as the Belvidere Council President for the town's League of United Latin American Citizens (LULAC) and was most recently appointed to the Ida Public Library board.

Nancy's bi-cultural background is conducive to community collaboration with the Belvidere mayor's office the local police and fire department. This has also led to provide for a number of volunteer opportunities, community leadership roles, and collaborative efforts with renown institutions within the Latino communities.

As a leader, Nancy sets the bar high for herself and goes beyond her words by living authentically and teaching others to do the same.

Nancy Razón
nrazon1981@gmail.com
(815) 519-1765

Blanca Sepulveda

"No matter where we are in life, there is always something new to learn and another level to achieve."

When I was invited to become a contributing author in this book, I doubted my accomplishments. Then I quickly realized that no matter where we are in life, there is always something new to learn and another level to achieve.

This story is about my journey and my gratitude in being where I am today.

FAMILY MEMORIES

My mother and grandmother gave me a loving foundation and were always great examples of hard work and resilience. My grandfather was a police officer in Mexico and was killed when my mom was very young. Once in the U.S., my grandmother worked as a full-time housekeeper at a hospital in Lake Forest, Illinois and on weekends, she cleaned beautiful homes in the area. She accomplished many of her goals. She owned a home in the U.S. and gave as much as she could to her children and grandchildren. She was always a great saver, forsaking instant gratification to fund her dream of building a house in Jalisco,

Mexico. She retired and moved into her custom-built house there, where she is enjoying life and keeping sharp by playing Rummikub, her favorite board game. She's very competitive and wins most of the games we play against her!

Three years ago, she was diagnosed with cancer. She is battling her disease in good spirits. She never complains and still has the memory of an elephant. She just turned 87, is still witty, clever, and loves to dance and be the life of the party.

My father worked full-time during the week and as a car mechanic on the weekends. He was a great influence on the family, always planning summer picnics at different parks and family trips to Michigan and Holy Hill, Wisconsin. He would gather carloads of relatives for these enjoyable family outings. He also always helped anyone in need and volunteered with the Red Cross.

I had my first glimpse of entrepreneurship from my mom. She was a beautician and was always making extra cash by babysitting, carpooling, baking cakes and making piñatas. Growing up, I really admired her. My parents divorced when I was 17 and my father left to start a new life and family. We felt betrayed, and it took us many years to forgive him. My mom quickly transitioned from being a stay-at-home mom to working full time and raising me and my younger sisters. I didn't want her to worry about me, so I quickly started working while I was in school.

I got a job as a teller in a bank, then became a customer service representative and continued working there while I finished high school and college. At the age of 22, I started working at the Federal Reserve Bank of Chicago, where I worked for 20 years. Around the same time, I was dating my high school sweetheart and found out I was pregnant. My whole world seemed to close in on me. I didn't want to get married; we had different goals in life. After a year, I decided to end the relationship with my baby's father and became a single mother. I planned to plant my flag at the bank, continue my education, and do the best I could. Over the years, my mom has been my biggest supporter and I will forever be grateful to her.

COMMUNITY ACTION

During high school, I got involved with my local community. My first meeting was with an organization called LOBO, Latinos of Berwyn and Cicero. I remember being young and learning about issues in our community and the importance of helping fellow Latinos.

When I turned 18, I registered to vote. I felt so empowered, I became a voter registrant. I would sit outside storefronts and walk around festivals urging people to register to vote to ensure they had a voice. I also got involved in immigration rights and went to Washington D.C. to attend my first protest. I didn't see myself pursuing a career in politics, but I thought it was important to be responsible, make a difference, and create a more powerful voice, together.

At the bank, I was involved in community outreach and helped start the bank's Employee Support Network Group, the Latino Resource Association (LRA). I was on the board for four years. I was also a volunteer for the United States Hispanic Leadership Institute (USHLI) annual conference for many years. Also, an organization that I still volunteer with, Junior Achievement (JA). Junior Achievement is a not-for-profit that goes into the schools and teaches students about money. Through JA, students learn about needs and wants, our communities, money, banking, economics, budgeting, starting a business, résumé building, and interviewing. I found the program fascinating and incredibly important. I taught students K-12 at the schools, then teach my son when I got home since he didn't have this program available at his school. JA will always be near and dear to my heart.

ENTREPRENEURSHIP

In 2012, I came across World Financial Group. I attended a personal finance workshop and heard about money concepts that I didn't really understand like the power of compound interest, paying less in taxes and assessing financial health. It reminded me of JA, but applied to the period after high school, when people start earning money and are making crucial money decisions. I realized there was still so much more to learn! Organizations like JA exist because there are no classes in school that teach us about money. There's English, math, social studies, science, etc., but what about budgeting, money 101, taxes 101, insurance 101 or how to use, not abuse, credit? Why don't these classes exist in our schools?

With the newfound concepts, I started crunching the numbers. I realized that my grandmother, who had worked hard, saved, and sacrificed all her life, could have had so much more. My family could have been more comfortable, spent more time together, and my parents would have fought less about money. I was disturbed as well as intrigued. I wanted to learn more, and of course, share this paramount information with my son, who had just turned 16 and started his first job. How I wished I was given all this knowledge when I was his age! We don't know what we don't know.

Today, I am so proud of him for implementing important financial strategies. How powerful it is to make a difference for the next generation! I am grateful to God that he will have a different, positive experience to pass on to his children someday.

Working in banking all my life had helped, but it wasn't enough. I remember being in debt as early as my 20's. Throughout my career, I've always worked two jobs, just like my parents did. I like to work, but I started asking myself, *why do we have to work so hard to get ahead in life? I can't do this forever. When do we spend time with family and do the things we love doing?* If we don't learn financial fundamentals we are all at risk. It's about working smart not hard.

I started questioning my position at the bank and found it wasn't rewarding. I wanted to be my own boss, help people, and make a lot of money, but that seemed farfetched. Where would I find such an ideal position? I thought I would need a big investment to get started, but I found that wasn't true. Through the WFG platform and guidance, I was able to start part-time so I would not have to immediately quit the bank.

I saw a demand to serve the community, sit down with families, free of charge, to educate, assess their needs, and go over their goals regardless of their income or savings. I believe everyone deserves the same courtesy, whether you want to invest $500K or $25 a month.

I also believe financial security is within reach for everyone. It doesn't matter if you just started your first job or if you are about to retire. Most people have questions about a 401k plan and how it works. How about a 403B? a 457? What funds should we pick within our plans? How do we save for our children's college? Or get out of debt? So many people need help and guidance with their retirement paperwork. Do you know your FIN? Your Financial Independence Number?

We are given decisions to make every day, decisions that will affect our future and our livelihood. Are we equipped to make these decisions? Are we taking advice from experienced professionals or our know-it-all relatives and co-workers who are just as broke and clueless? Do people really want to work past 65? Do people work because the want to or because they have to?

After learning and becoming skilled at following a simple system, I wholeheartedly made the decision to leave my career at the Federal Reserve Bank. I have never looked back!

The average financial advisor is male and in his 50's, but now the baby boomer generation will be retiring and there is a tremendous shortage of financial advisors. The industry is growing, and it's very diverse now. I'm excited to see an increasing number of women enter financial services. According to the Department of Labor, the profession is projected to grow 15 percent from 2016 to 2026, much faster than the average for all occupations. As the population ages and life expectancies rise, demand for financial planning services should increase too. I plan to be there, helping those who need help the most.

ENCOURAGING SUCCESS

In life, we will always have our ups and downs. I suddenly found myself at a crossroads. I had so much to be grateful for but still felt empty and stagnant. I began growing in my faith and learned that everything God has destined for us is right in front of us, but we are often so busy or worried that we don't see it. Sometimes it's fear that's stopping us from moving forward. I was afraid of disappointing people. I was ready for the next stage in my career, to grow an agency but didn't feel like I was knowledgeable enough or good enough to lead others. It was a lack of confidence that held me back.

I've learned that as long as we focus on becoming a better version of ourselves and working hard in all aspects of our lives, we will gain the confidence we need to grow. God will always be there to pick us up when we fall or fail, no matter what the circumstances. I am stronger, braver, and more grateful for the people God has placed in my life. God is good. If you ask Him, He will guide you. He will open your eyes. We just have to be true to ourselves and take action in the little things in order to grow.

My team is like my family. I want to help them reach their personal goals as well as make a difference in our communities together. We are opening offices all over the Chicagoland area, suburbs, and across the U.S. I would like to see my offices in every city, the way we see banks throughout every community.

With faith and resilience, we will conquer fear and overcome any adversity. I want to see other women rise and break free as well. I want them to know that yes, they are qualified; we are all worthy.

It's important to surround yourself with people who lift you higher and help you excel. I have met some great people who have helped me along my journey, and I want to do the same for others. I thank God for my mentors and friends who are always rooting for me.

Finally, I'd like to thank all the women out there, empowering and cheering for one another. Women are leaders, and in the right environment, we uncover the gifts God has in store for us. He wants us to make our dreams come true, but He wants us to take others with us on this journey as well!

REFLECTION

1. What do you feel when you think about money? Do you feel confident?

2. If you have children, do you think you have taught them everything important to you?

3. How do you give back to the community?

BIOGRAPHY

Blanca has worked in the banking industry throughout her career and spent 20 years at the Federal Reserve Bank of Chicago. She is passionate about giving back to the community and has since become an independent financial professional working with the largest, most well-respected financial firms in the industry. She went to Morton Community College in Cicero and DePaul University Chicago Loop.

Blanca is involved in many volunteering efforts and has worked with organizations that include Junior Achievement Chicago, Association for Latino Professionals for America (ALPFA), Prospanica's SEP Summer Enrichment Program, The Rotary Club, The Resurrection Project and Community Support Services (CSS). She is excited to have recently become a part of the Fig Factor Foundation as a mentor to young Latinas. Blanca continues to partner up with many community-based organizations to bring financial awareness and implement financial strategies and solutions for families and individuals.

Blanca Sepulveda
blancasepulveda17@gmail.com
(708) 426-9024

Laura Muller

"Learn to be smart for life. Find something at which you excel."

It was six o'clock in the morning and our professor agreed to meet us in front of the university cafeteria for class. My friend and I waited calmly, complaining that it was an indecent time to turn in work, while a girl from another class waited, leaning against a wall and smoking one cigarette after another. When the professor approached, he called the girl and said, "You shouldn't be smoking so early; you're going to get cancer." To which she replied, all the while looking me up and down, "I would rather die of cancer than die from being fat."

Her words were nothing new to me. Since I was a child, people have referred to me as "fat." What was new was hearing someone say they would rather die of cancer than look like me.

That day, I got into my car and cried all the way home. My heart hurt. It hurt to be alive. I felt like I had been torn to pieces. I had little dignity left. I wanted so deeply to disappear from the world, to cease to exist, to stop suffering for something that I had been feeling since childhood. The girl who was smoking preferred to go bald, suffer unimaginable pain, and die rather than look like me.

FAT, UGLY, AND DUMB?

In kindergarten, I was very happy. I never realized that I was different. I felt free. I played, sang, and participated in activities. However, everything changed when I entered elementary school. On my first day of class, I was received by my classmates who told me I had a pig's nose, I was shaped like a ball, and I was fat, ugly, and dumb. I was called so many names it felt like a daily struggle to get through the next day, to wake up when the alarm clock went off at seven o'clock and prepare myself to once again be humiliated to the center of my core. And that's how I felt...fat, ugly, dumb, useless, slow... exactly the words my classmates used to taunt me every day.

When I see pictures of myself as a young girl, I think "I wasn't even that fat!" I was very big and tall, much taller than other girls my age, and that in itself made me different. And being different was the worst thing that could happen to me.

I spent my daily recess breaks in the school library. I didn't want to go out because the other children would not include me in their games like hide-and-seek or cops and robbers. They told me I was too slow and I would make them lose. They rejected me all the time. For example, I was sent to the back of the classroom because I was too tall and I had to let the shorter children see. Always being placed in the back, combined with my attention deficit diagnosis, had disastrous effects on my ability to learn and retain the lessons.

So while the kids went out to play during recess, I would take my turkey sandwich and sliced cucumbers to the library and devour the "diet lunch" my mom prepared for me. She was worried I wouldn't lose weight. While at the library, I also devoured books by Jules Verne and the *Encyclopedia of the Treasure of Youth*. I met Rider Haggard and his stories, and became a literature aficionado. All this reading helped me develop a bigger vocabulary than any other child in my age group.

However, feeling so ugly, useless, and despised at such an early age had harsh consequences. Several times I thought about suicide, but I never tried it because it scared me. I used to come home heartbroken after school, gather my dolls and my black kitten named Cleo, and go to bed telling her she was my only friend. She didn't care if I was fat, ugly, and dumb.

I managed to survive my childhood by belonging to a group of Boy Scouts. At that time in Mexico, there were no Girl Scouts. We were all Boy Scouts and scouting taught me the love of nature, how to physically challenge myself, how to be a leader and gave me a place where I was respected and where I was Laura, not just that fat girl. It was a place that allowed me to develop my leadership skills and learn the joy and satisfaction of doing things well and providing service to others.

After elementary school, things were not at all easy regarding my weight. My relationship with food became harmful... very harmful. I learned to eat with fear. I learned to eat for revenge. I learned to eat on the sly. I learned to eat when I was feeling anxious.

I was determined to not let eating define me. As a person, I was much more than that and I had many qualities I could develop through my studies. In 2005, I was invited to participate in the World Youth Congress in Sterling, Scotland where I met young people from all over the world who were involved in social issues like me. Later, that experience helped take me to several countries as a lecturer.

I finished my university studies at the top of my class after being labeled "dumb" in elementary school. As a child, I clearly remember my mother repeating to me, "Laura, learn to be smart for life. You don't have to be smart for school. You are going to find something at which you excel." And so I did!

MISSIONS ACCOMPLISHED

I began to write a Sunday column called Urban Roulette for the Mexican Publishing Organization, one of the biggest newspaper chains in Mexico. The column was later published as a book under the same name. That work, and my journey supporting social causes, earned me the Peace Ambassadorial Scholarship of the Rotary Foundation, which led me to study a postgraduate degree in journalism in New Zealand. Professional success followed and it was a part of my life in which I felt complete, but there was always the shadow of being overweight.

When I turned 30, I reflected on my achievements and realized I had reached many of my goals. I had a book published, a postgraduate degree, and had traveled for more than two months backpacking through Asia and Oceania. Yet in the background, all I had wanted my whole life was to have a normal body, to be a thin person. I felt that all of my accomplishments and ambitions were a cover up for the insults I endured for not being thin.

I gave everything up. I left my safe and well-paying job. I left my newspaper column. I left an invitation for an all-expense paid trip to Turkey to cover an event as a journalist. I left it all to dedicate myself to what I had always wanted... to be able to buy a standard size of clothes and feel what it would be like to be thin.

It hurt my soul to leave the safety of professional success, but I am a goal-oriented person and I knew I had to do it. I found a self-help group that helped me learn how to cook healthy meals. I met people like me who had suffered the consequences of being overweight and who at that time, just like me, were struggling with what I learned was an emotional illness. About a year later, I had lost 110 pounds! And even though I had been told I would never be able to fit into a size eight because of my structure, I was able to fit into a size four.

I cannot explain the happiness I felt when I wore a bikini for the first time. And it didn't matter that losing so many pounds had consequences on my skin. I just felt so full, so happy, so fulfilled. That was Laura... Laura in a normal body.

It was during that time period that people started asking me what I had done to lose weight. In Chicago, I started supporting people who were struggling with weight loss through a self-help group. At the same time, I started uploading videos to YouTube to teach people how to eat healthy. Only those of us who have suffered from being overweight know how frustrating it is to visit a doctor who tells you, "Stop eating tortillas, stop eating bread, stop eating sugar and you're going to lose weight." The process is much more difficult than that. It's a physical problem with very strong consequences and emotional ties.

LIVING WITH WEIGHT LOSS

Soon, my YouTube channel and social networks began to grow, and my husband joined the project. To date, we see this as a way to support people like me who have had to face the problem of obesity. I dedicated myself not only to sharing recipes, but also to talking openly about my pain and struggle with obesity, looking for ways to support parents who have children with this problem and telling them about my experience so they can help their children as well.

Currently, I reach more than 1.8 million followers through my social networks. It has been a beautiful path that has taken me to places I never imagined. I was invited to Washington for the Partnership for a Healthier America Conference with Michelle Obama, nominated as one of the most influential Latinas in the United States, and invited to tell my life story for Disney Princess at one of their conferences in California. These are just a few examples of my many wonderful adventures.

For five years, I managed to stay thin. It was a constant struggle between me and my metabolism. I could not eat more than 1,400 calories per day, and I had to commit to two hours of daily exercise. My life had become almost 100 percent dedicated to staying thin. It was exhausting, and I was suffering too. Many times I cried because I was hungry, but I knew that if I ate one orange too many, the scale would destroy me the next time I weighed myself.

When my husband and I decided to have a baby, I went into crisis mode. I was not sure I wanted to be a mom. I was afraid that my son would go through what I had gone through as a child. I asked myself, what if he is fat? *What if they make fun of him?* I also knew that the priority would no longer be me and that I would not have the time to stay thin.

Today I have two healthy and beautiful children. My struggle with being overweight returned and the daily challenge of focusing on my health continues. Some days I win and other days I lose, but I don't give up.

Today I don't feel that I am starting from scratch. I no longer insult myself in the mirror. I try to be patient with myself in this process and honestly, sometimes I go into difficult stages where I hate my metabolism and I feel very tired of always being on a diet and always feeling fat, but I know that I can't give up.

Today I know that I am more than a number on the scale and my worst defect has become my best ally. Today I am able to serve others and keep me and my family eating natural and healthy foods. The challenge continues as I commit to lose any weight I gain. My goal is not to be a size four again but probably a healthy size 12.

Life is not perfect. When your own devils attack through depression and bad self-esteem, just remember to be thankful for the things you have. You have arms to carry your kids, legs to stand up every morning, and loved ones to fight for. We'll always have challenges but if we change our flaws into our ally, we can prevail!

REFLECTION

1. Are you smart for school or for life?

2. How can you make what you hate about yourself into your ally?

3. Do you face your struggle with joy and hope?

BIOGRAPHY

Laura Muller is a Radio Claret America news anchor and journalist. She is also a mom of two boys and has two cats and a husband. Her mission is to show a real face of motherhood while also sharing information and healthy recipes to enjoy as a family to keep loved ones healthy.

As an influencer, Laura shares the value of maintaining Hispanic roots by encouraging bilingual and bicultural families to promote family values in unity. Laura also shares her life with more than 1.8 million people via her social media channels.

Laura's healthy recipes program has taken her to Washington, D.C. with Michelle Obama's Partnership for a Healthier America. She has also been a speaker for a Disney Princess conference in California.

Laura has worked with Walmart, Gerber, Barilla, Dole, Disney and many other brands. With Radio Claret America, sharing sensitive information in Spanish as well as radio programs focused on self-esteem and spiritual growth.

Laura has a degree in communications with a postgraduate degree in journalism from the University of Canterbury. She is a published author of *Urban Roulette* and *Healthy Recipes*. She has also completed postgraduate studies in right to information and in domestic violence and gender equity.

Laura Muller
info@lasrecetasdelaura.com
(773) 517-3560

Maribel Guerrero

"When you show someone their value, you can transform their life."

Walking across the stage to receive my bachelor's degree from Aurora University was one of the most inspiring days of my life. As I held my well-earned diploma in education in my hand, I looked into the audience at my mother and father's faces and felt truly empowered. That day I realized that if you dream it, you can do it. I was inspired and motivated to start teaching. I remember thinking, what can stop me now? My dream of helping my family was in motion, even though I had been helping them from a very early age. I have always wanted to help empower others, even as I have empowered myself.

LEADING THE FAMILY

Growing up in Aurora, our household spoke Spanish. My parents had immigrated to the U.S. from Durango, Mexico in search of a better place to raise their family. Being raised in Aurora was like never leaving Mexico. We still continued traditions, spent time with family, and the community was very welcoming. Being the eldest and the first-generation here, I had to help my parents navigate life in their new country. At the age of ten I was often my parent's translator for doctor appointments, teacher conferences, retail shopping, and anything else they needed. I felt pressure to learn the language quickly.

My mother was the heart of the family and my father was a hardworking man who provided for us. Their work ethic and determination set an example for me to follow and shaped me into the person I am today. I witnessed their sacrifice for us and through their perseverance and ceaseless labor, I learned that nothing is impossible in this life.

In school, I was not the most outgoing student and was often shy and embarrassed to speak up. I was worried about my accent and whether I would say things correctly. Sometimes learning English seemed overwhelming.

I clearly remember a moment during class when a teacher asked me, "What do you want to be when you grow up?" I had never thought about it; I saw college as an unattainable goal, but I knew deep inside that I loved working with children, and I would spend hours playing *la escuelita* with my sisters. I looked at my teacher and replied, "I want to be a teacher." He immediately looked at me and said, "One day I will be driving through a fast food drive thru and YOU will be the one to take my order." At that moment, all I could think was how can my teacher expect so little of me? I clearly remember him saying similar things to the rest of the class too. I wondered how a teacher that is expected to guide and motivate students could expect nothing from us?

Since that day, I decided not to let anyone's expectations of me influence how I performed. I kept telling myself I would make my parents proud and be sure to succeed. My parents didn't speak or understand English, but my mother always made sure she was involved in school conferences and she checked our grades and made sure we did our homework. Education was very important to them.

Some of our family members would tell my parents that our schools were substandard, and we would not get a good education. My mother's response was always, "The school doesn't matter; it is the student and what that student wants to do about it."

As the years passed and it was time to graduate high school, I knew I had to make a decision. It was either go to college or work in a factory. My mother advised me to work in the factory to help with bills. Something inside of me kept saying, Maribel you can do more. I decided to apply for college, without even knowing how to do it or what the process was. I just knew I wanted to start the journey.

My parents were worried and knew that money would be the big obstacle. I promised them that the only money I would ask for was the 100 dollars for the application. I applied and received a scholarship that covered most of my undergraduate tuition. I also had a full-time job to cover books and other school fees. My parent's continuous struggle motivated me to continue, even in the hardest days, to stay up late finishing homework and to get up in the morning and head to school. I wanted to demonstrate to them that it was possible for us to get an education, something they did not have the opportunity to do. In under four years, I graduated with a degree in elementary education.

Because I graduated in December, I expected to have difficulty finding a job because most graduating teachers would already have a yearly teaching contract. Thanks to being bilingual however, I found a teaching job as a Dual Language teacher in Barrington, Illinois. It was the first time I had heard about Dual Language and was very intrigued with the concept of having students embrace both the Spanish and English language. I worked there for five years and had the opportunity to teach many grade levels.

FOR THE LOVE OF FAMILY

Unfortunately, a few months after I started, I received horrible news. My mother had been diagnosed with stage four metastatic cancer. It was March 25, 2009, a day like any other for most people, but for me it was the worst day ever. In front of me, with tears in her eyes, my mother looked at me and took her last breath. Before doing so, she made me promise I would take care of and look out for my two younger sisters. I remember asking *WHY? WHY GOD?* My heart broke into pieces. My mother, my best friend and motivator, was gone.

For years I did not share how painful it was for me to not have my mother alongside me in the journey of life. I was only 21 and filled with dreams--dreams that now seemed impossible to achieve through such pain. I had no choice but to silence the pain and be strong for my family.

In these darkest hours, I called upon my faith in God to help me when I felt alone and had no support from anyone. I was forced to forget my feelings in order to get things done. I shared my happiness, accomplishments, and dreams with my sisters; but at times I needed to share my doubts and sadness with someone else and I never had anyone for that. However, God seemed to open a door when I felt everything was closed. I would find myself filled with energy and vibes of positivity when I thought everything was lost.

Ultimately, I dedicated my time to work, school, and family. I felt the only thing I could do was become a good role model for my sisters and make sure they had all they needed to succeed. I returned to school to pursue my master's degree. Being a positive mentor for them was not only a responsibility, but a choice. I wanted to inspire them to continue with their education and make sure they knew that I would always support them. But I also knew that I needed to become financially stable in order to help them out.

I started looking for a job closer to Aurora so I could help care for my sisters. I searched for a teaching job closer to home and found a job opening in Naperville, Illinois for a second grade Dual Language teacher.

I went on to enroll in Aurora's doctorate program, since I believe that teaching requires us to be lifelong learners. Many called me crazy and some even told me I wouldn't be able to accomplish it. But I did. At age 30, I became Dr. Maribel Guerrero! As I walked across the stage for the third time at

Aurora University, I realized teaching was my passion and empowering Latinos was my mission.

I felt empowered and knew I could now make an even bigger impact on teachers and youth. I had been seen only as a bilingual teacher in my district, but I decided to apply for a position outside of Dual Language. I knew it would be difficult and it was, but I persevered.

I am now a learning support coach working with teachers for professional development, implementing streamlined data collection and promoting data-informed and responsive teaching practices. In the summer, I am a professor at Roosevelt University where I teach a few courses for the Masters in Dual Language Teacher Leadership program.

I love the position I am in right now because everything I do empowers teachers to believe in themselves. I have grown in my listening skills. I listen to teacher's ideas and help them structure their ideas into a potential plan. I am often quoted saying "Do it, I'll help you," as I see their potential unfold and we push together to make it happen. I make sure that they do not fail, and if we do fail, we fail together.

TEACHING WITH IMPACT

Today, I empower students as a teacher, I empower teachers as a coach, and I empower whoever is around me because that is the person I am. My work is not just my job; it's my life. I support not only the learning of my students and teachers but also their emotional well-being as they work through challenges.

I firmly believe that when you show someone their value, you can transform their life. I also believe in acknowledging the importance of all the people I meet, and this position gives me that opportunity.

All nestled into a career I love, I've taken time to really dig deeply into finding my passion. What do I want to be known for? I know I'm passionate about empowering Latinos. I want them to know that anything is possible when you take action to reach your goals and you should never let stereotypes and barriers stop you from achieving your dreams. I want them to embrace their driving passion to achieve their vision.

Parents, students and staff now regard me as a student and family advocate and to that end, I was excited to recently be awarded a grant entitled, "Engaging and Empowering Hispanic Families through Culturally Responsive Collaboration." The grant is to support Hispanic families in helping their students achieve by providing them with services, resources, and parent education

I tell young people to not give up and fight for what they want. I tell them many will discourage, doubt, and question you, but ultimately the one in charge of your life is you. By having a growth mindset, you can accomplish anything with hard work.

My sisters went on to school themselves. One of my sisters is a registered nurse at Copley hospital in the medical surgical/oncology department where she treats and gives care to cancer patients. The other is a health tech at a school and a cosmetologist. They tell me they see me as the most "powerful" woman in their life. They see me as a role model and second mother who has guided them in the right path, the one that cheers, consoles, and forgives them. They say I'm the one they admire for my ability to overcome obstacles. I'm the one who has answers to every single problem they have and tries to help them look beyond their barriers.

God has been a huge part of this journey by being my strength to continue and not give up. I believe there is a mission for everyone. God is always with us even when we think we're alone.

I don't let circumstances or obstacles determine my success; instead, I focus my will to achieve goals and objectives which will move my vision forward and achieve desired results. I want to ignite that same passion in others. *¡Porque juntos logramos la diferencia!*

REFLECTION

1. Are you smart for school or for life?
2. How can you make what you hate about yourself into your ally?
3. Do you face your struggle with joy and hope?

BIOGRAPHY

Maribel Guerrero, EdD, is a first-generation, Mexican-American who was born and raised in Aurora, Illinois. She is committed to student success inside the classroom and in life.

Maribel is a Learning Support Coach with Naperville District 203 and is passionate about helping students become bilingual, bicultural, and biliterate. She assists teachers in their professional development as needed, implementing effective instructional practices to ensure high academic achievement for all students, increasing individual and collective teacher capacity, and leading change. Her work within the educational system has earned her a grant to support Hispanic families in helping their students achieve.

Maribel holds a Ed.D in Curriculum and Instruction and is a part-time professor at Roosevelt University where she teaches courses for the Masters in Dual Language Teacher Leadership Program. She dreams of one day having her own educational consulting business that will help school districts create the best possible learning environment for one-way or two-way dual language programs to graduate successful bilingual, bicultural and biliterate members of society. She is an avid runner and recently completed her first half marathon.

Maribel Guerrero
marybelg27@yahoo.com
(630) 442-3958

OUT OF THE DARK AND INTO THE LOVE

Miriam Gaeta

"Love comes from within."

A wrong decree, a fantasy world inside a closet, a mistaken idea of happiness and an uncontrollable impulse to flee far away from reality were all hallmarks of my life and helped show my path to success.

Within my own home, I experienced the terror of early psychological abuse. I was raised by my grandparents since my mother was very young and couldn't take care of me. In the beginning, I felt protected and beloved, just like all happy children. Later, a visit from my great grandmother, who spent time alone with my grandpa, changed my entire story.

After that, I couldn't figure out why my grandfather suddenly hated me, or so it seemed. The gas can, which was stored in the service room, became the focus of threats against my grandmother and me. "I will burn you up while you're sleeping if you don't behave," he would say.

My ensuing panic made me a child who opted for silence. At school I didn't speak. I couldn't interact with a world that was hurting me and I didn't want to, either. I dreamed of flying away to a different, wondrous, and happy life.

My grandfather finally kicked me out of his house and told me I had to live with my mother instead. He said I had to go where I belonged now that my mother was married again. However, even though the household freaked me out, I felt I belonged there. My grandma had taken care of me since I was a little girl and she was my only family. I now had to build a space where I could feel safe, forget my fear, and be out of my grandpa's sight.

I created a fantasy world full of all the things I imagined, lit only by a small lamp illuminating my childhood thoughts. There inside a small closet, I imagined I was in a movie as the main character. I left my grandfather's abuse behind that closet door. I couldn't get out and my world was inside that small space, nothing else.

My grandmother's apparent submission to grandpa's plans made it almost impossible for her to defend me. I know she cried when I was at school, and she would leave home to walk aimlessly, just trying to clear her mind and find a solution or a door able to take us out of hell.

After several years, grandma finally left my grandfather. But I still thought of escaping even though we lived without him in a different, peaceful house.

WAY TO FREEDOM

Danger passed by. My grandfather's yoke and the risk of being burned alive while sleeping was left behind like a nightmare after waking.

When I was 17 and in high school, I started working as a model. Thanks to some friends, one year later I had the opportunity to travel to Germany as part of a student exchange program. I soon turned 18, and my dreams were huge. I had awakened to the reality I always wanted to live and was no longer inside that closet.

I wanted to know the whole world, lead a normal life, find the perfect mate, and raise a family. My grandmother taught me that the role of a woman was to please the man, and I wanted to follow that example. Back then, I didn't know anything about happiness.

After one year in Germany, I went back to Guadalajara and had my first boyfriend, but our relationship failed. He wasn't ready to start a family, so I couldn't fulfill one of my main goals with him. Instead, I studied foreign trade and graduated, still thinking about going somewhere else.

I realized I didn't want to live in Mexico anymore. I had a dream and it was just beginning. I decided to move to Chicago in the United States. There, I started materializing those old childhood stories. I became a photographer, since I had studied photography in high school. While in Germany, I learned that a woman could be independent of a manand it helped strengthen and encourage me to fulfill my goals.

IN SEARCH OF SELF-LOVE

In pursuing my idea of happiness, I was able to travel around the world several times. I visited Tokyo, Dubai, Shanghai,

Mongolia, Singapore, India, Thailand, Croatia, Italy, Paris, Sweden Peru, Brazil, Jamaica and other major countries of the world. I realized you can achieve anything if you really want it with your heart.

Desire can become reality. An example of that started with apencil and paper in my journal as a child. I hadn't found the perfect man who I thought would make me happy, even as I searched for him around the world. One day, I was in Bodh Gaya, the Buddhism Holy City where Prince Siddharta became Buddha. There, in the Himalayas, I wrote a letter witnessing my deep desire to meet the ideal person. On paper, I described the perfect man in my imagination, exactly how I wanted him.

Later on, this desire materialized at the Monaco Grand Prix, a famous race of the most prestigious and oldest Formula 1 cars. "My dream man" was finally a reality. In my letter I wrote that I wanted a successful, loving man, among other things, who allowed me to focus on what I care about. Just as I asked for him, life sent him to me. But I did not find happiness.

I remember the day perfectly. I was staying in the Hotel Presidente in México City to visit my "perfect" man, and he was working again. Naturally, he was too busy to be with me since he was indeed the busy man I had envisioned! So there I was, alone and unhappy.

I was enjoying a relaxing massage when I had an epiphany. I knew happiness and fulfillment were not to be found in another person, but inside me. Love comes from within. So what happened with that ideal man I met in Monaco?

I fell in love... with myself.

I found happiness once I started living in the present and fell in love with myself. The yoga and meditation that I had learned in the Himalayas was now fundamental for me to leave behind the hurt of the past. But falling in love with oneself does not happen in a moment, or even in a day. It is a process, a path, which can be challenging, but must always be traveled.

With the knowledge I had gained from the sacred places I had visited and the people that life introduced to me, I was living the way I had always dreamed I could live. I took pictures and planned events, but the only thing I really needed was to just love everything that I am. I loved myself with a true love.

I got into the habit of taking better care of my body and spirit and thinking mainly of my own welfare. I ate healthy food and worked out as I always did, but now it became a discipline, because loving yourself is a discipline.

I realized that when you are filled with problems, insecurities, fears, and annoyance, you infect others with it and they reject you. On the other hand, when you are happy, satisfied, smiling and excited, life fills you up with what you need. You surround yourself with wonderful people and goodness will flow around you. I now see with crystal clear clarity that this is what I needed, and nothing else.

I learned that all the happiness I had always wanted was right inside me. Loving me as I do now, I steadily try to fulfill my expectations of myself. I am blessed to have special people in my life. Manny, my brother from different parents, has been an example of love and compassion. My lovely son, Nicolas, has helped me realize true unconditional love. He is handsome, intelligent and fun.

Of course there's nothing wrong with material goods. Having a beautiful home, a Ferrari, being fashionable, having a good man, and a family are worthy goals. Nevertheless, having all of these, without loving yourself first, will not make you happy. Loving others, without loving yourself first, isn't love at all.

THE JOY OF HAPPINESS

Finding myself happy and fulfilled about every aspect in my life, I'm able to realize that other people's happiness also pushes me forward.

At first, I chose photography because I wanted to capture all the beauty of the world. Later, with my event planning business, I realized that simply seeing people smile also brings me great joy.

My experience has given me strength to encourage the women who experience violence at home, work, or in daily life, to seek refuge from their situation. Sometimes women think the violence will stop. Sometimes they are not compatible with their partner anymore and are just trying to keep the family together. However, we all have the right to happiness and the right to achieve it. The moment you divide the world into right and wrong, into God and devil, your love becomes very conditional. It becomes enslaved to external situations and it will no longer be quality, but something that will only happen because someone or something else is wonderful.

Love is not about someone else; it is your quality. Just as

health is of the body and happiness is of the mind, love is your emotion.

Love is your quality. You are just using things and people around you as stimuli to find expression for this quality. If you bring sufficient awareness to the discriminatory intellect, loving is the only way you can be. Love is not what you do. Love is what you are.

BIOGRAPHY

Miriam Gaeta is an event planner, wedding and "quinces" specialist who loves to put a smile on every client's face. In 2012, she founded Gaeta Lovely images, her Chicago-based photography business. She also works as an international photographer for Vision3, a company based in California, which specializes in photography for international projects around the world. She is quadlingual, with proficiency in German and Italian in addition to Spanish and English.

Miriam has been working as a model since she was 17 years old and she was an exchange student at Edertalschule Frankenberg High School in Germany. She graduated with a degree in foreign trade from Universidad Marista de Guadalajara and in photography from the Instituto Cabañas, Guadalajara, Mexico. She seeks continuing education in photography, with her latest coursework completed in San Francisco, California.

Miriam trained as a yoga instructor at the International Yoga Alliance in Tuscany, Italy. She also recently completed training with mystic Sadhguru in Los Angeles, California to become certified as a coach in the inner engineering program, a form of spiritual guidance. Since December 2008, Miriam has led the non-profit organization, Love is Still the Answer, which benefits orphan children.

Miriam Gaeta Ron
miriamgaetaron@gmail.com
(773) 712-0644

Claudia Ayala

"Sisterhood is the base."

I was at a national convention in Los Angeles, training on how to organize a community campaign for the Little Village Environmental Justice Organization (LVEJO) back in Chicago, when I heard the words that would change my life: "Nothing about us, without us."

I had just quit my comfortable job as an AT&T sales representative, which was supporting myself and my two children. "You'll make less money at this job, but you'll be able to spend more time with your kids," Selene Gonzales, the charismatic, LVEJO leader told me. She was right too. With every campaign, I was able to have my little lion cubs right beside me.

When I asked the speaker what "Nothing about us, without us" meant, he told me, "If an issue is impacting our community, make sure you have a voice. Don't let others represent you or speak for you." The topics discussed that day included politics, environmental justice, climate justice, transit justice, food justice, politics. It made me realize the power of organizing, social capital, and narrative.

That was almost a decade ago. Since then, I have lived by

that quote, challenging the status quo as an unapologetically brown and confident Latina, both kicking down doors of social injustice and knocking on the doors of diverse neighborhoods with various needs. It takes a direct and authentic approach to engage communities to understand issues and organize for real results.

THE POWER OF SISTERHOOD

Identity is very personal to me. Throughout my years at the frontlines of grassroots movements meeting people from every background, gender, and fusion, I now find the definition of identity, and how it is defined, to be very important.

Growing up in Chicago and surrounding towns, I have been influenced by the diversity of many cultures and life experiences. My livelihood has always depended on identity and connections. I learned to get to know people and how they identify themselves. I learned to connect deeply and quickly, even with customers.

Like many other Latinas, my earliest memories of identity as a Mexican woman came from my mother. She was the first "professional power woman" I ever saw, and I so wanted to be like her, challenging expectations and proving that women can be anything they want to be at anytime in their lives.

My mother had been a teacher, and an independent, young, single mother with a degree, raising me in Mexico City. After meeting and marrying my father, who lived in the United States, they decided to raise their family there. Initially, her teaching degree was not valid in the U.S., but she would not give up her identity as a working woman. Many family members urged her to compromise her ambitions. "Let your husband work and you focus on your family," they would say. Instead, she wanted to contribute and succeed, rather than just survive, so she decided to become a journalist, which was a career too dangerous to pursue in Mexico.

From watching television, she quickly acquired a vast knowledge of the Mexican telenovelas, the soap operas of the Spanish-speaking channels, so she pitched a gossip column to one of the local media outlets. She got the job and for no one else but herself. Her success impacted me and helped drive me forward in my goals, many years later. She taught me that our identity, and our belief in what we can accomplish, is significant to our success.

As I grew older and became an unmarried, working mother, raising two kids from a former relationship with another powerful Latina, Edna Flores, I learned that our identities are forever changing and evolving. We must constantly be in tune with change, who we are, and what we want to become. My identity is very different than my mother's, but my resiliency springs from her ability to define her identity through what she did, not how she was perceived. I established my own identity as someone who speaks for herself and knows her worth.

Another driving force for me, especially in the past decade, has been the concept of "sisterhood," especially among fellow Latinas. Throughout my career, the women I have met have helped me develop from that twenty-something, getting-herself-together, trying-to-make- ends-meet single mom into a confident, social juggernaut, woman's advocate, political strategist, campaign field operations professional, union organizer, and partner of Edna. Things are looking up because I refuse to keep my head down. I know that sisterhood requires us to pick each other up. We must stay afloat and let others help us.

My long-pursued bachelor's degree in psychology is within reach and I now think ahead instead of taking one day at a time. I still have those days when I am just trying to get through. But now I have the incredible blessing of meeting, working, and advocating with strong and opinionated women of all economic and ethnic backgrounds. They assist me in my quest for equality in economic achievement, health, and political advocacy.

Just prior to that day I stood in the convention hall, I had freshly witnessed my LVEJO friends, including Selene, achieve a historic victory. She had helped lead the initiative to shut down a polluting coal plant in Little Village, a predominantly Hispanic-populated area in Chicago. I had never witnessed anything like that before. Until then, I was all about survival: paying my rent, raising my children, and making money. This was a kind of different survival.

The training at the Los Angeles Strategy Center at the conference, my brothers and sisters fighting a cause, the communities where I organize, and the political campaigns I have served have all changed my life. They have made me realize the power of information, relationships, and most of all, how important it is to have a seat at the table and a narrative you can control and share with others.

VICTORIES AND THE VILLAGE

When I first started volunteering with LVEJO, I wrote their blog and translated their printed information. Once I came aboard, I was asked to assume a campaign from my predecessor, Mike Pitula. The goal was to reinstate the 31st Street, number 35 bus whose route had been cut by the Chicago Transit Authority (CTA). The loss of the number 35 produced a transit desert, leaving 90,000 people in several communities without reliable, safe transportation in an area often riddled with gang violence. It also affected many children who relied on the bus for safe transportation to school.

Mike had the challenge of connecting with the residents of Little Village as an Anglo-organizer. When he left LVEJO, he handed the project to me. "This is my baby," he said. "Take good care of it." How happy and proud I was when within eight months of successful talks with the CTA, we were able to get the route reestablished! I had delivered the baby in one term!

After that victory, I become unshakeable. I had found my gift to the world. I was a connector and a communicator, able to reach many people and children in a real and authentic way. The twenty-year-old saleswoman developed into something bigger and set out to do something other than struggle to survive. Organizing woke me up, and that is the journey I have been on.

I took on unfamiliar roles every chance I could, organizing for school choice with the soccer moms or Gage Park, Brighton Park, Back of the Yards neighborhoods and Chicago's Southside. I successfully campaigned for the formation of *La Villita Park*, a badly needed, new greenspace in Little Village, and I have worked with some of the fiercest women I have ever met in my life. I have been part of field operations, doing political advocacy, and campaigning with the Amalgamated Transit Union, Local 241.

During the 2008 presidential election, I helped Congresswoman Tammy Duckworth on the campaign trail in Cleveland, translating her literature into Spanish at a time that wasn't done. On election night, we saw the state of Ohio turn a victorious blue color for the first time ever!

I was there when Chicago hosted the NATO (North Atlantic Treaty Organization) summit in 2012 and community organizers from around the city gathered outside the Daley Center to focus international media attention on the most important local issues. Because of my 31st street bus work and my support of a recent teacher's strike, the Chicago Teacher's Union (CTU) asked me to address the gathered community about the challenges facing education. I addressed the crowd in Spanish to demonstrate that Latinos are a powerful, thriving force, both in and outside of Little Village.

I have helped more than 13 local, state, and county political races. I have learned that sisterhood is the base, with power at all levels to create a positive impact on our external and internal environments. Sisterhood is fostered by women's intuition, a powerful tool in any effort.

MOVING FORWARD

As I meet different people, I realize our stories are seldom told as is. They're "polished" to get rid of everything unique. I also notice the power of social media to voice and control your narrative, so I began to use the hashtag #theclaudiachronicles to symbolize the need to tell a story our way, as it unfolds in my bird's eye view. My visual Instagram blog captures selfies, outings, and wins, but also my family and partner Edna, who is very private, but very important in my life. Besides my children we have raised together, who are a true source of pride, Edna has constantly inspired me to raise the bar. I am grounded by the way she humbly achieves her goals. My sister, Fabiola, as well as my cousins (who are like sisters) Nayelli, Ana, and Patty, all ground me.

To expand this circle, I launched The Goaldiggers Club in October of 2018. It's a women's advocacy group focused on redefining our personal narratives through the mind (career mentorship), body (health and mental wellness), and soul (empowerment and self-care/advocacy). I still find myself on a journey, always evolving and proud to be at the frontlines of these women's movements, including *Today's Inspired Latina*. Everything feels like it's coming full circle. There's no stopping us now.

People have asked me what I want to achieve from all this activism. It took me a long time to answer that question, but I want to work towards a more equitable world, where gender equality is the norm. I consider myself a feminist, but I do not support non-inclusive or derisive feminism. With women's rights and advocacy issues, my goal is to include ALL women, including women of color. We have been surviving and helping one another for some time, but have much to teach each other if and when we are given a voice, a platform, or an opportunity.

I look forward to creating, connecting, and catapulting women to their highest potential. But I don't think I look forward to anything more than seeing my children graduate and grow into respectable, fearless, kind, and confident Mexican-American individuals, raised by two determined Mexican women, traditional in our values and radical in our love for one another and our commitment to helping each other rise.

The work I do is not glamorous. The fight is hard and there are no rainbows or lollipops at day's end. But it is all worthwhile and important to use your gifts to create a better world.

Currently, I serve Chicago as a strategic Latina community engagement consultant. I am vice president of Local 1041 in my hometown of Berwyn, and a member organizer with AFSCME Council 31, as well as a community and building development facilitator. Every chance I get, I work on the Goaldigger's Club, creating events and actions to promote our mission. It's important to find your voice and use it, especially when issues concern you. And that's why I do what I do and how I hope #theclaudiachronicles will impact the world

REFLECTION

1. Has anyone ever used words against you? How did you react?

2. Have you ever taken a leap of faith? Who did you trust to help you?

3. Do you see adversity as a positive or negative thing?

BIOGRAPHY

Claudia Ayala is award-winning community organizer who has led many grassroots and political campaigns at both the local and national level as a citizen, advocate, political advisor and strategist.

Claudia immigrated to the U.S. from Mexico City and experienced the challenges young women of color faced in the footprints of environmental injustice and discrimination at an early age. She created personal resilience to overcome these social challenges and has helped others voice the cultural, psychological, and social struggles of those directly impacted by issues such as job access, women's rights, choice of body, education choice, LGTB rights, labor disputes, and inclusion and diversity causes and campaigns.

Claudia Ayala is the Founder of Goaldiggers Club, Chicago, a group of women self-defining their identity. She captures her experience through her hashtag #theclaudiachronicles and independent podcast appearances and blogs. Recently, she has been honored for her leadership by the State of Illinois, Little Village in Chicago, the Metropolitan Leadership Institute, and the City of Berwyn.

She is currently the vice president of her Local 1041, a union organizer with AFSCME Council 31, and is pursuing a bachelor's degree in psychology. She lives with her two children and Edna, her life partner.

Claudia Ayala
cea@goaldiggersclubchicago.com
(312) 792-4406

Karla Vazquez

"Challenges in life are inevitable, but defeat is up to you."

Last summer, I attended a Hispanic leadership conference in Chicago, where I currently live. There I met an incredible woman who had an amazing story about how she made her way up the ranks at Goldman Sachs while being undocumented. She was successful, but also lived in fear, thinking she'd get caught at any moment.

As she addressed the audience about her journey and where she is now, she asked us to close our eyes and think back to ten years ago. "Think about where you were then, and where you are right now. Did you ever imagine you'd be here?" she asked the crowd. My heart filled with joy as my eyes welled up with tears. I couldn't believe where I was ten years ago compared to today.

AMERICAN OPPORTUNITY

I was born and raised in Monterrey, Nuevo Leon, Mexico with two younger sisters and three, older half-siblings who I love deeply. My family is devoutly Catholic, so I personally grew up admiring Pope John Paul II, not only for his position, but for his incredible talent with languages. I wanted so badly to be able to communicate with the whole world the way he could! It was that deep desire that kept me in America after a family visit.

I was 12 years old, visiting with my family as a tourist to celebrate my cousin's Quinceañera. I had visited America before when I was younger, but this time the two-week visit was like a dream. It was summer and I simply loved being in Chicago. I didn't expect the trip to alter my life forever, yet it did when my aunt suggested we extend our visit. My parents would not think of it; they had jobs and a life back in Mexico. However, on the day before we were to return home, they sat me down.

"Karlita, what do you think about staying here and going to school?" they asked.

"YES!" I didn't give it a second thought; this was my opportunity! Imagine, learning a new language, going to school here, oh the possibilities! Possibilities I knew I would probably never have back in Mexico.

My parents were shocked. "*Segura?* (are you sure?)" they asked. I repeated my answer. "*Bueno,* you can stay, but you can come home whenever you want."

I thank God and my parents for allowing me to make such a monumental decision on my own. It wasn't easy; my family struggled with the psychological and emotional struggles of separation and my mom felt guilty for letting her little girl live so far away from her. Back home, my little sisters cried and missed me so much that my dad bought the family a puppy to help fill the void. He would spend hours videotaping family activities so I would not miss a second of their lives when we reunited.

I suffered too because although I stayed with family, they were strangers to me. My aunt was going through a divorce, and she spent most weeknights out with her friends, dancing her sorrows away. My cousins were older, so they only stopped by the house occasionally. The cousin closest to my age was not kind to me. I spent most of my days alone in the house after walking myself to and from school, just a couple of blocks away.

As with many other immigrants, sacrifices had to be made in order to make ends meet when my parents finally moved to the U.S. My parents gave up life as medical professionals to be office janitors. Their goal for me was the same as mine-- get an education and go to college.

COLLEGE BLUES

When the time came to apply, I was hit hard by the reality that I expected but had yet to face. If you haven't guessed by now, like the girl at the beginning of my story, I too am a Dreamer, an undocumented immigrant. And as if the college application process isn't excruciating enough, I had to navigate the process with little help or hope.

You see, I was about to graduate third in my class with a couple of Advanced Placement (AP) classes and community college courses under my belt, and there was no way I was not going to go to college. I had heard stories of people like me going to freaking Harvard on a full scholarship! If they could do it, what made me so different?!

I worked hard in school, stayed out of trouble, and did

everything I was told to do in order to succeed. My status shouldn't have been an obstacle. But time and time again, it was. Never in my life was I bombarded with as many "no's" as I was my junior and senior year of high school. It was crushing, lonely, disappointing and defeating.

When I sat with the college counselor of my high school and laid out my college choices – Harvard, Northwestern University, University of Chicago, Loyola University, Washington University in St. Louis-- she stopped me a few minutes into our meeting and said, "Perhaps you need to lower your expectations. Your situation may not allow it," she continued. Allow it?! She then proceeded to list a couple of city community colleges as my best options. I was outraged. There's nothing wrong with community college for some people but didn't she see my credentials? Wasn't she supposed to encourage me to reach for the stars?

I was determined to find another way. I kept applying to other colleges and when the inevitable acceptance letters began to pour in, another reality hit me. *How am I going to pay for this?!* I had won several thousand dollars in scholarships, but nowhere near the amount I needed. I learned of a nationally recognized, politically involved Latino organization that claimed to be dedicated to the advancement of the Latino community. I visited their office in the Little Village neighborhood of Chicago and asked for their help with funding. I was told, yet again, to lower my expectations. "Perhaps it's best you ride out 'your situation' and think about working as a waitress or something that would pay under the table until Congress acts," they said.

I felt sick to my stomach. I couldn't believe my ears. I walked out of there, got into my dad's car and told him the bad news. Panic began to set in. Could I pull this off? Alone?

A couple of weeks later, I was told by my counselor that some of the top students in my class were eligible for a college scholarship, and I was one of them. When I went to her office to apply for the award, I was told I needed to provide a social security number. I was at my wit's end.

As I walked back to my AP class, I stopped cold at the door frame and collapsed in the hallway with tears streaming down my face. My best friend rushed to my side as she tried to hold me up, and I wailed, "I'm not going to college, I'm not going to college!" "Yes, you will! Yes, you will," she kept telling me. I felt hope leaving my body; I couldn't see my future anymore. I was filled with desperation, anger, loneliness. What could I do? I was a teenager and I seemed to be failing this rite of passage into adulthood.

With a heavy and aching heart, I watched my dad lose sleep over my struggle. He even proposed we reach out to our state senator or representative. Then one day, the high school heard I had no plans to attend college. In their vain attempt to claim 100 percent college acceptance, they connected me to the admissions director of my now alma mater.

I reluctantly visited the campus with my parents, two weeks before the semester began. When I set my eyes on those large grass fields and the majestic water fountain, I fell in love. The director was warm and empathetic and on that day, he not only gave us hope, but awarded me the Presidential Scholarship. Along with my other small private scholarships, I was set. My dreams were coming to life again.

I majored in international business, French, and studied pre-med. I met amazing friends and was able to live the college life I had always envisioned.

My story doesn't end there. When graduation rolled around in 2008, my prospects were not good and my undocumented status only made things worse. This time, I saw the roller coaster coming, but unlike the first time, I felt numb. I tried to fight, but again the "no's" were too loud. For many years, I just lived, waiting for something to change. I did volunteer work and even returned to school and earned an MBA in Finance so I wouldn't have a gap in my resume when the opportunity finally came. But I was lost, living without direction and purpose.

In June of 2012, my life was changed yet again, thanks to President Obama and DACA (Deferred Action for Childhood Arrivals). My fighting spirit returned; it was as if I were a phoenix rising from the ashes. This time no one could stop me. I'd been through so much that I was overcome by a sense of invincibility.

KEYS TO SUCCESS

I was 30 years old when I began my career and today, I work as an investment associate in Asset Management, surrounded by a group of talented and successful people I could only imagine working with in my wildest dreams. Through the ups and downs, there were three things that kept me going and I want to share them with you.

First, many people say to "trust your gut," "trust your instinct," or "trust yourself," but I'd like to suggest to just remain true to yourself. Whenever I was true to who I am, what I stood for, what I wanted, what I liked and didn't like, I made decisions that I will never regret, even if the outcome was not what I desired.

Second, be grateful because when you are grateful, you are happy, and when you are happy, you feel motivated. When you are motivated, you feel compelled to act, and good things can happen.

Third, there will be those that judge you by your circumstances and not by your potential. Don't let that defeat you. That's their loss.

Now, close your eyes and think back ten years ago and where you were then. Now think about today and where you are now. When you feel defeated, frustrated, hopeless, alone, and afraid as I did, just remember, challenges in life are inevitable but defeat is up to you.

REFLECTION

1. What keeps you going in life?

2. How do you handle it when you keep hearing "no's" to something you want?

3. Will you be led by your circumstances or by your potential?

BIOGRAPHY

Karla Vazquez is the Investment Associate for the Investment Advisory Practice (IAP) team at Northern Trust Asset Management (NTAM), providing service and support to the investment and sales professionals within the Wealth Management business pertaining to NTAM's registered investment products.

Prior to joining the IAP team, Karla was a Senior Representative in the Client Implementation and Transition Services team at Northern Trust. Prior to joining Northern Trust, she worked for the Law Offices of John F. Shine.

Karla holds a *Series 7 and 63*, is a CFA level II candidate, and is a member of CFA (Chartered Financial Analyst) Society of Chicago. She is an officer, board member of the Latino Resource Council at Northern Trust, and co-chairs their professional development committee. Karla holds a B.S. in International Business and in French from Elmhurst College, where she graduated cum laude. She also holds an MBA with a focus in Finance from Saint Xavier University, where she graduated with honors. She is a member of Sigma Lambda Gamma Sorority, Inc.

Her newly legal, resident retired parents, her two younger sisters, and her 17-year-old poodle named Chikis (or as she calls him, "my precious") are everything to her!

Karla Vazquez
kvazquez23@gmail.com
(773) 841-1389

Jackie Camacho-Ruíz

**ENTREPRENEUR, AUTHOR, SPEAKER, PHILANTHROPIST,
TODAY'S INSPIRED LATINA FOUNDER.**

Jacqueline Camacho-Ruíz is an award-winning entrepreneur, international speaker, philanthropist and author of many books, including The Little Book of Business Secrets that work published in 2010. She is the founder of The Fig Factor Foundation focused on unleashing the amazing in young Latinas. Jacqueline is a regular guest on local and national TV, radio and print publications.

She has received many prestigious awards for her business acumen and impact in community, including "Influential Women in Business Award," "Entrepreneurial Excellence" Award and "Annual Awards for Business Excellence" by *Daily Herald Business Ledger*, "Best Under 40" by *Suburban Life*, "Unsung Hero" by the *City of Aurora* and "Woman of Distinction" by *Kane County Magazine*. As a two-time cancer survivor, Jacqueline possesses wisdom about life well beyond her years. She lives in the Midwest with her husband and business partner, Juan Pablo Ruíz, and her two children. In her spare time, Jackie enjoys flying airplanes, racing cars and experiencing the beauty of life.

For more information, visit www.jackiecamacho.com